PENNSYLVANIA DUTCH COUNTRY
GHOSTS
LEGENDS AND LORE

BY
CHARLES J. ADAMS III

EXETER HOUSE BOOKS
Reading, Pennsylvania
1994

PENNSYLVANIA DUTCH COUNTRY
GHOSTS, LEGENDS AND LORE
©1994 Charles J. Adams III
Published by EXETER HOUSE BOOKS

Portions of this book have been adapted and/or excerpted, with permission, from *Ghost
Stories of Berks County*, *Lehigh Valley Ghost Stories* and *Berks the Bizarre*, other publications
of EXETER HOUSE BOOKS.

FIRST EDITION
PRINTED IN THE UNITED STATES OF AMERICA

ISBN 1-880683-03-2

TABLE OF CONTENTS

INTRODUCTION

Imagine a society...a world...a time...without ghosts.

Imagine a life without Ebenezer Scrooge and his Christmas Carol demons...Imagine no Shoeless Joe Jackson emerging from the high Iowa corn into a Field of Dreams...Imagine no one ever uttering words such as these:

I AM THY FATHER'S SPIRIT; DOOMED FOR A CERTAIN TERM TO WALK THE NIGHT, AND FOR THE DAY CONFINED TO FAST IN FIRES, TILL THE FOUL CRIMES DONE IN MY DAYS OF NATURE ARE BURNT AND PURGED AWAY....TIS NOW THE VERY WITCHING TIME OF NIGHT WHEN CHURCHYARDS YAWN, AND HELL ITSELF BREATHES OUT!......

The words are those of William Shakespeare.

From the bard of Avon to the ball yard of Iowa, the supernatural...and, as the ancient Scottish prayer warned–ghoulies and ghosties and long-leggety beasties and things that go bump in the night...have twisted their unsettling images into our literature, our music, our art, our films, our theater, and indeed our very beings.

Who among us has not shivered with wild and wide eyes as a ghost story was spun before a crackling fire?

Who among us has not read Poe, or Dickens, or King (or Adams) beneath a single lamp on a stormy night and has not fended off goose bumps?

Who of us can offer proof positive that somehow, somewhere, on some other plane or in some parallel time, we do *not* share our world with spirits...specters...with

I

phantoms...with *ghosts*?

Do ghosts exist? Do you–do I–believe in ghosts?

Do *clouds* exist? Clouds we can see, but we cannot touch them, we cannot capture them in jars.

Does the *wind* exist? Wind we cannot see, but we can feel it as a gentle breeze or a terrifying blast.

Do I, as one who chronicles the carryings-on of these ghoulies and ghosties, believe in those ghoulies and ghosties?

Does it matter?

One must face the reality of death, and therefore I believe one must face the proposition that while the human *animal* must perish, the human *animus* may indeed remain. What was flesh and bone may become dust. But, what were electrical charges in the nervous system may continue as information-laden impulses which stay, suspended and circulating in an eternal swirl of a magnetic field.

Could these impulses–shards of emotions and information from a now-dead body–then record themselves somehow on something? As in simple tape recording, could not these invisible pulses possibly become attracted to and deposited on rust?

Could these scientifically-rational and conceivable electrical charges which burst from their corporeal confines at the time of extreme trauma be the seeds of the supernatural? Could these bits and pieces be *ghosts*?

If there is one thread which weaves its way through nearly every tale I have investigated, it is that on virtually every "case," the building in which the haunting took or is taking place has been renovated or altered in some way.

Could any kind of severe trauma–such as, but not limited to, death–which may have taken place in those places have resulted in those impulses bursting from the body, and the recording of those impulses on rust? Could the renovation have disturbed that recording by

2

exposing the rust and allowing an unwary psychic mind to push the "play-back" button and detect these impulses?

As inconceivable as this may be to some, so is the proposition that faces and forms and voices and sounds could be recorded on strips of rust-coated plastic and retrieved on a glass screen or paper speaker.

Such are the mysteries of the world we call the supernatural, and the wonders we call ghosts.

As Edgar Allan Poe wrote in his "Spirits of the Dead":

THY SOUL SHALL FIND ITSELF ALONE
ALONE OF ALL ON EARTH, UNKNOWN
THE CAUSE, BUT NONE ARE NEAR TO PRY
INTO THINE HOUR OF SECRECY.

BE SILENT IN THAT SOLITUDE,
WHICH IS NOT LONELINESS, FOR THEN
THE SPIRITS OF THE DEAD, WHO STOOD
IN LIFE BEFORE THEE, ARE AGAIN
IN DEATH AROUND THEE, AND THEIR WILL
SHALL THEN O'ERSHADOW THEE.
BE STILL.

Charles J. Adams III
Reading, Pennsylvania
Walpurgis Nacht
April 30, 1994

✣✣✣

FOREWORD

Perhaps the most difficult thing about writing about the Pennsylvania Dutch Country is *defining* the Pennsylvania Dutch Country.

Geographically, we defer to parameters set by William N. Hoffman in his excellent travel guide, "Going Dutch."

Hoffman extended the "Dutch Country" from Franklin County in the southwest to Northampton County in the northeast. In between, all or parts of Adams, Cumberland, York, Dauphin, Lebanon, Lancaster, Berks, Chester, Montgomery, Bucks and Lehigh counties joined the aforementioned two in Hoffman's definition.

He stated the PDC, as he called it, sprawled over 7,100 square miles, just slightly smaller than New Jersey.

Anyone who lives in the region knows there is really no Dutch Country as such. If anything at all, it is the Pennsylvania German Country.

But, try telling that to the person of Italian, Polish, Welsh, English, Spanish, African or any of the other diverse ethnic backgrounds which make up the people of this storied "Dutch Country."

Still more accurately, it is the Pennsylvania *Deutsch* Country. Deutsch, of course, meaning German. And, it is the corruption of that word which led to the misplaced moniker, "Dutch."

What is now Pennsylvania was home to the Lenni Lenape, Conestoga and other Indian tribes long before

4

white Europeans settled. The colony was established by the British, but first settled by Swedes.

The Germans came in large numbers, and the land between the Susquehanna and Delaware Rivers and south of the Blue Mountains did indeed become a "Deutsch Country" of a sort.

While the principal counties of what we shall conveniently call the "Dutch Country" are Lancaster, Berks and York–each named for English "shires," their earliest populations were predominantly German in extraction.

These so-called "Engellanders"–Quakers and Anglicans–held hard to the economic and political power bases during the years of early development, but their German neighbors stood steadfast in the retention of their proud culture.

While the common perception by many visitors to the "Pennsylvania Dutch Country" is that it–whatever *it* may be–is centered in Lancaster County, nothing could be farther from the truth.

A 1993 report by the Pennsylvania State Data Center at Pennsylvania State University Harrisburg Campus revealed that Lancaster County is not even in the top five counties which could be considered "Pennsylvania German" when based on the ethnic origin of its people.

Using information collected by the U.S. Census Bureau, the Data Center extrapolated that Carbon County had the highest proportion of those who could be considered Pennsylvania Germans.

Following Carbon, which listed 6.6 percent of its population as having Pennsylvania German ancestry was Lehigh County (5.8 percent), Northampton (5.2 percent), Columbia (5.0 percent) and Berks (4.6 percent).

Lehigh County reported the most (16,995) residents of Pennsylvania Dutch heritage. Next in total number were Berks, Northampton, Montgomery and

Bucks Counties.

The Census Bureau considers those who claim Amish, Mennonite, Hutterite and the generic "Pennsylvania Dutch" ancestry as being Pennsylvania German.

Still, for the millions of tourists who flock to Lancaster County every year, it is the heart of Pennsylvania Dutch Country. It is also the focal point of these tales.

The area which is the present-day Lancaster County was settled in about 1709 by Swiss Mennonites and Scots-Irish.

Twenty years later those who homesteaded in what was then the western fringe of sprawling Chester County complained that they were too far removed from the seat of their government.

A successful petition to the colonial government resulted in the partitioning of that frontier and the establishment of a county called Lancaster.

Then, it spread north and east to the Schuylkill, north and west to the foothills of the Appalachians, and far beyond the Susquehanna River.

In ensuing years, all or portions of what are now Berks, Lebanon, York and Dauphin counties were trimmed from Lancaster.

As the natives of the land ceded that land to the settlers, the natural attributes of the region contributed to its steady growth.

The town of Lancaster once served as capital of the Commonwealth, and for one day as the federal records and their keepers fled Philadelphia when a British attack seemed imminent, the town was the official capital of the United States.

After the Revolution, as Congress sought a new and permanent seat of the federal government, Lancaster, York and Wright's Ferry (now Columbia) tossed their municipal hats in the ring.

6

Internecine squabbling between supporters of each town's cause resulted in the selection of none. The capitol dome rose over the Potomac, not the Susquehanna.

But it was–and is–the *people* of the "Pennsylvania Dutch Country" who primed the pumps of progress over the centuries.

James Hamilton, who established the two-square mile plot which would become Lancaster city, was still in his twenties when he did so.

James Buchanan, Thaddeus Stevens, Robert Fulton–each in their own way gave their talents to Lancaster and the nation.

A deeper dig into the rich history of Lancaster and the other counties of the "Dutch Country" will readily reveal valuable contributions of men and women of all races, religions and ethnic origins.

That bountiful cornucopia of diversity in art, architecture, language–and the supernatural–has remained very strong over the centuries, and it is really all of those influences we celebrate in this book.

Let it be ascertained from the start that this volume is not a history book.

It is a compendium of folk tales, legends, lore, and the real stories of real people. It brings together for the first time a sheaf of tales which were hitherto spread across broad and elusive sources.

Thus, what you are about to read falls not within the exacting bounds of the historian or the folklorist. It is a book for the rest of us–those of us who enjoy a good ghost story.

I hope you will find enjoyment in these pages.

Perhaps you will learn something about this magical and mysterious land.

Perhaps you will find that the "Dutch Country" is more than a haphazard hodgepodge of shopping centers, ersatz quaintness and a windmill, bank barn and buggy-bedecked "people zoo."

Better yet, perhaps you will feel the hair on the back of your neck stiffen....your skin tingle....and have that frightening feeling that somebody is standing over your shoulder, peering down at you.

Now–right now, turn around! Anyone there?

Are you sure?

Sleep tight tonight!

‡

TALES OF HEXES, WITCHES AND WIZARDS

In many senses, the Pennsylvania Dutch Country is a world apart from the rest of the state and nation.

Its food, its art and architecture, its language and dialects, its customs and superstitions—all contribute to the charm and the singularity of this fascinating region.

The area is also a wellspring of American history and folklore.

In Lancaster and surrounding counties, those two elements are so intertwined that they become weaved tightly into a braid of fact, fiction and fantasy.

To understand the breadth and depth of the ethereal side of life (and *afterlife*) in the Dutch Country, one must consider the strong and solid foundation upon which the supernatural superstructure has been built.

The footers of that foundation are sunken deeply in the traditions of the natives who lived on the land before the first settlers.

More directly related to modern culture, however, are the beliefs brought by the Europeans who populated the area in the eighteenth century.

Most notable among those beliefs and customs was the art of "powwowing."

Still today, some old-line "Dutchmen" still visit powwow doctors before consulting a physician in even the gravest matters of health.

These "powwow" doctors, or faith healers, were most prominent in the nineteenth century, but their influence remained strong into the 1900s.

In a 1904 edition of the *Journal of American Folklore* , Carleton F. Brown wrote, "Among the Pennsylvania Dutch, the 'plain folk' such as the Amish, the Dunkards, and the Mennonites, as well as the 'church people,' the Lutherans and German Reformed, the Pow-Wow doctor has a large following."

Even into the latter part of the twentieth century, powwowing is practiced in the Pennsylvania Dutch Country to a degree which, in 1984, sent the Pennsylvania Board of Medical Education and Licensure to look into just how widespread that practice was.

The board found that there were more practitioners and patients of powwowing than anyone had estimated.

Lawyers for the board sought to separate the charlatans from what could be called honest powwowers.

Their probe went deep into Lancaster, Berks, Lebanon and other counties of the Dutch Country.

They found that there was a fair amount of chicanery among those who used powwow as a cover for less sincere and forthright healers.

The investigators trod on delicate legal ground.

In 1893, the state medical laws were written with a provision which allowed powwowers to practice freely and within the bounds of those laws, as long as they did not prescribe medication, misrepresent their alleged cures or require fees.

In essence, the lawmakers turned the other legal cheek at what they thought was an innocuous practice of faith-healing.

Scholars are split in their assessment of powwowing. Some call it an art, some a science. Some say it was—and is—apart from any supernatural connotations.

Carleton Brown said, "The Pow-Wow practitioner is more closely allied with theology than medicine."

However, in the 1977 book, *American Folklore,*

10

author Richard M. Dorson referred to the powwow doctor as a "shaman figure," and powwowing as an "occult art."

In an unattributed article in the November 10, 1827 *Philadelphia Gazette,* powwowing was dismissed as "the offspring of an erroneous and vicious education, imbibed from nursery tales of ghosts and visions, and also from false religious notions."

The account continued:

> *Powwowing is a regular and well established business in the interior. Our readers are aware that this powwowing is what is designated in English as charming.*
>
> *The process is, making certain gestures, turning round, moving the hands backwards and forwards, repeating certain words, etc.*

The writer also strays from powwowing, but provides a bizarre bit of information about the protective value of a hangman's noose:

> *In the interior of our own country, the virtues of a rope with which a malefactor has been hung, are well established; and it never fails to afford a pretty perquisite to the hangman.*
>
> *It is usually sold in small portions of an inch or two in length, and he that gets a piece carries it home in triumph, and with full faith that his family, his cattle, and his property will be protected from many dire afflictions.*

In his research, Richard M. Dorson also offers a root for the word itself, asserting that "powwow" is derived from "powaw," an Indian word for "enchantment and witchcraft." Some Indian shamans were also called powaws, and were reputed to have the power to tell fortunes and heal.

The early German settlers in Pennsylvania called the healing art "braucha" or "braucherei," and it is generally believed that their English neighbors were the first to dub it "paw-waw" or "powwow." Some scholars propose that the word came from the misunderstood, German-accented pronunciation of "power."

Another curious phrase used to describe those with the "power" was that they were "able to do more than eat bread."

In the thin ranks of publications which are directly related to powwowing, three stand out. One has direct connections to the Pennsylvania Dutch Country.

It was written not by a man of letters or medicine, but by an itinerant artist.

The man was as much a mystery and enigma as his legacy.

Precious little is known about his life. What he left for all eternity to ponder is cloaked in a shadowy realm between what is natural and what is *super*natural.

He could be considered what his legacy was entitled: *Der Lang Verbogene Freund*, or "The Long Lost Friend."

He was Johann Georg Hohmann, and to practitioners of powwow, he was a master craftsman and chronicler.

It has been fairly well documented that Hohmann was born in Germany in 1775.

At age 27, he emigrated to the United States, landing in Philadelphia with his wife, Catherine, and son, Caspar. They came in indentured servitude and were purchased by a Bucks County family.

To pay off his debts, Hohmann wandered throughout southeastern Pennsylvania, trading his calligraphic and artistic talents for sustenance and cash.

He illustrated, illuminated and lettered family

documents, and was said to have been skilled at the intricate art form known as fraktur. His main source of income was from "taufscheins," a form of illuminated baptismal certificates.

A devout Catholic, Hohmann collected prayers, potions and superstitions along his way.

By 1819, his own philosophy and theology became tightly intertwined with the eclectic sampling of cures, curses and verses he had gathered in his itinerancy.

Just how he came to actually publish his own book is unknown. But, in 1819, hoping for financial and spiritual gain, "The Long Lost Friend" was printed and distributed.

Published in German, the book emerged from a press somewhere in Berks County. Early editions indicate it was published on "July 31, 1819, at Rosenthal, near Reading."

It is believed Hohmann may have had access to a printing press and may have done the job by himself. This factual gap in his story is but one of many.

A rambling mixture of thoughts and processes gleaned from such diverse sources as the Hebrew cabala, Egyptian hieroglyphics and the deep mysticism of the Germans, the Gypsies and the Druids, "The Long Lost Friend" circulated quietly in the underground of early nineteenth century society.

It offered strange cures, protections and precautions. Some believed it was a manual of hexes, curses and spells. One contemporary newspaper article called the book "rude and uncouth." Another reference linked the cures with Satanic worship. Hohmann vigorously denied that accusation.

Indeed, he at once offered bold claims as to the potency of his work and firm apologies and explanations as to its benignancy.

Its frontispiece was all-inclusive:

The Long Lost Friend
Containing
Mysterious and invaluable
arts and remedies
for
man as well as animals
With many proofs of their
virtue and efficacy in
healing diseases. etc.

And, the last page of the book provided a brash declaration:

Whoever carries this book with him is safe from all his enemies. visible or invisible: and whoever has this book with him cannot die without the Holy Corpse of Jesus Christ. nor drowned in any water. nor burn up in any fire. nor can any unjust sentence be passed upon him. So help me.

Hohman did not mince words in his preface. Among his assertions:

•I say: Any and every man who knowingly neglects using this book in saving the eye. or the leg. or any other limb of his fellow man. is guilty of the loss of such limb. and thus commits a sin. by which he may forfeit to himself all hope of salvation.
•I have given many proofs of the usefulness of this book. and I could yet do it at any time. I sell my books publicly. and not secretly as other mystical books are sold.

Hohmann presented four pages of "testimonials"

from individuals who, he said, would vouch for the powers of his healing techniques.

He also gave a brazen hint as to the sources of some of the cures and remedies and his motivation for publishing the book:

•This book is partly derived from a work published by a Gypsy. and partly from secret writings. and collected with much pain and trouble. from all parts of the world. at different periods by the author. I did not wish to publish it: my wife. also. was opposed to its publication: but my compassion for my suffering fellow-men was too strong. And I therefore ask thee again. oh friend. male or female. is it not to my everlasting praise that I have had such books printed? Do I not deserve the rewards of God for it?

The most widely circulated edition of the book measured three by five inches, and spread over 128 pages, including a ten-page index.

What is remarkable about Hohmann's thin volume is that it has not been out of print since the day it was first released. The first edition in English was published around 1855. Reprints of reprints are still available in gift and book shops throughout the "Dutch Country."

In 1928, the book gained certain notoriety when it figured in the "Hex Murder" of York County.

A man who felt he had been cursed by another determined that the only way to break the curse was to steal the other's copy of "The Long Lost Friend."

The aggrieved man wound up killing the alleged "witch" instead. An account of the murder, and the ghost which accompanies it, follows in this book.

Hohmann never realized any real monetary gain from his effort. Six years after the book was published, his modest farm went under the sheriff's gavel.

Hohmann's book is considered either an historic novelty or a hornbook of healing, depending on the reader's outlook.

No matter, the curative offerings make for interesting reading.

Consider Hohmann's remedy for hair loss: "Pound up peach kernels, mix with vinegar and put on the bald place."

Or, for warts, try roasting chicken feet and rubbing the warts with them. Then, bury the roasted feet under the eaves of your home.

A simple precaution against injuries is to carry the right eye of a wolf inside your right sleeve.

Some cures had curious codicils.

In his "Remedy for Epilepsy, Provided the Subject Had Never Fallen Into Fire or Water," Hohmann suggested the victim write "IT IS ALL OVER" backwards on paper one time.

They then must put the paper in a scarlet cloth and wrap it in unbleached linen. *Then*, they must hang the bundle around their neck on the first Friday of the New Moon.

The books suggested ways to catch bigger fish, to cure worms (in both men and cattle), and to ease ailments ranging from toothaches to tapeworms.

Sometimes, there were options.

To stop bleeding, either recite, "Jesus Christ, dearest blood, that stoppeth the pain and stoppeth the blood," or count backward from 50. When the number three is reached, Hohmann said, the bleeding will stop.

Among the most baffling, and yet the simplest, of the remedies is one for the sniffles.

"Whenever you pull off your shoes and stockings, run your fingers in between all the toes and smell it. This will certainly effect a cure."

Uh, yeah!

There are those who have probed far deeper into

Hohmann's life and legend who feel they have either tied up loose ends or untied tangled knots of misinformation.

These historians are to be lauded for their work, and that work should be added to the relatively scant information which has been recorded about the man's life and labors.

While little has been documented about Hohmann, he remains one of the most intriguing figures in the long, dark shadow cast by history.

Another book which was usually found in the library of all powwowers is the Sixth and Seventh Books of Moses, or as it was published in the region, "Sechstes und siebentes Buch Mosis."

Researcher Ammon Monroe Aurand theorized that the book is based on magic and cures Moses learned while he lived in the house of the Pharaoh.

Again, the book contains mystical incantations, prayers, and magic symbols.

The third book which is a reference for healers and practitioners of powwowing is "Egyptian Secrets," a three-volume set by Albertus Magnus.

There have been a handful of other publications which suggested treatments and powwow procedures. Most were published privately and distributed on a very limited basis.

One "hex book" warned that a cow's udder can be bewitched by "mischievous elfic spirits" which could well be disguised as something as innocuous as a toad.

"Toads are suspected of sucking the teats through evil influences or as the incorporation of evil forces," the anonymous author claimed. "Here, however, the thief is really the elf or witch in animal form. There is quite a common belief that if a toad is killed the cows will give bloody milk."

Various methods in dealing with bovine disorders, including the aforementioned "Dievel's Dreck," are offered, as is the following rather specific set of

17

instructions:

If cattle are reluctant to enter the stable,
as if afraid of someone who is turning them away, take an old
skull of a horse, and wood that has been washed out by water, and
nine hazel heads. These three items must be gathered in the
morning before sunrise, wholly unbeshrewed, put in a little box and
buried under the doorsill. You may add nine grains of caraway, as
much salt, nine crumbs of bread and a little asafoetida. Your
cattle will then be safe from all evil, especially if you perform the
above on Good Friday or Easter Sunday.

Even more bizarre was the cure for a bewitched
horse, as offered in a pamphlet published in Ephrata,
Lancaster County, in the late 18th century:

Take the bones of a dead person, from the cemetery, and a piece of
wood that has been washed out by water. Then, take an earthen
pot and pour into it a quart of vinegar and add a few scrapings of
the bone and of the wood. Stir well with the wood and then pour
into the horse's mouth, making him hold his head up so that he will
swallow all of it. Bleed him at the shoulder vein. Tie some of the
bone and of the wood on the right side under the mane. Return the
rest of the bone and of the wood to the place where you got them.

Some of the cures were downright vindictive. One
way to remove warts (a common viral target of
powwowers) was to require the afflicted individual to
bring a whip to the healing session.

The powwower would dig three notches in the whip
handle and instruct the patient to take the whip to the
closest place where two roads intersect and place it there.

The wart would be transferred to whoever happened to come by and pick up the whip.

Another remedy for warts was fairly common: Rub a piece of raw potato over the wart and then bury the potato under the eaves of an outhouse. As the potato rotted, so did the wart.

Superstition played a strong role in the powwow formulas for treatment and prevention.

It was believed by some folks that if they walked barefooted all day Good Friday, they could do so all summer and never suffer a foot injury from a thorn or sharp stone.

Those who washed their feet in a bucket and did not toss the wash water away would find dead chickens in the hen house the following morning.

If a fork was dropped in the kitchen, a male visitor would soon come. If a knife fell, a female would visit.

If an individual had hiccups, they could try thinking of a church and a school house and naming them aloud. As they did, their hiccups would cease.

There are as many myths as their are truths about the practice of powwowing.

In its classic form, it is so secretive that few on the outside are privy to the complicated (and somewhat arbitrary) way a person *becomes* a powwower.

Theoretically, the practice was only passed down within a family, and strictly from one sex to another. This male/female/male/female transfer of the "powers" has been called *crossways*. In these more enlightened years, however, as powwowing has faded into folklore, those with the powers have eased their once strict admission policies.

There are reports of healers passing their secrets on to those of the same sex, and outside the nuclear family. Just as a powwower does not solicit business, he or she cannot solicit a student. One must ask to be taught, and must meet tight criteria to be accepted into the fold.

This sort of thing has actually been going on for many decades, but has been cleverly disguised by a rather interesting technique.

A powwower who desired to pass on the rudiments of the practice to someone not of the family or of the same sex would actually pass on the information to an inanimate object such as a chair or table, while the "student" would be in close earshot. The student would then pick up the information indirectly, and the "teacher" would have stayed within the accepted bounds of secrecy and formality.

There actually is little formality to powwowing. Among the more famous powwowers in Lancaster County history are Charles "Doc" Dubson and Israel Widder. Both used diverse methods in their "healing."

Before his death in 1940, Dubson would treat as many as 100 patients a day in his prime. He powwowed only two days a week, and took on customers from several counties.

Dubson, a former vaudeville acrobat and nurseryman, specialized in magnetism. He would place his hands a few inches above the afflicted person's body and draw the malady from them. In a flash, he would flap his hands, and cast the demons, the virus, or whatever, into the wind.

Widder, who lived near Ephrata, was in practice around the turn of the 20th century. He drew his cures from Hohmann's book, but also based much of his philosophy on the Christian Science teachings of Mary Baker Eddy.

Some say this folk medicine, this faith healing, this braucherei, this *powwowing* is a form of witchcraft.

Indeed, even some of its practitioners admit there is a certain "white witchcraft" employed in the course of powwow healing.

In Pennsylvania German folklore, witchcraft translates loosely as "hexerei."

This emerges most popularly in the form of "hex signs" which are sold in gift shops throughout the "Dutch Country."

In this supposedly more sophisticated age, these colorful signs are dismissed as mere barn decorations and harmless folk art.

Some researchers, however, claim the different designs on the signs were very significant to early farmers.

Some were thought to protect crops, family and property; some were designed to invite fertility; and some were placed on a barn or outbuilding to ward off devils and demons.

The hex sign was but one form of art used in that more superstitious era.

Also employed to cast away evil spirits were so-called Devil's Doors and Witches' Windows. Basically, they were fake windows and doors painted on barns. The hope was that the dimwitted demons would believe the false apertures to be real, and attempt to enter the barn through them. Instead, they would be knocked unconscious or, at least, repelled by the trickery.

Less obvious to the casual visitor to Lancaster, Berks, Lebanon, York and surrounding counties are the places which bear names and associations with hexerei and witchcraft.

As far east as in Northampton County, just south of Easton, is "Hexenkopf," a cluster of rocks in Williams Township, near Raubsville.

Even in the twentieth century, there are those who will blame their misfortunes on the antics of the witches who dwell in the rocks of the hill whose name translates to Witches' Head.

Poking more than 800 feet over Stout's Valley, the hill's mysteries can also be traced to the old German beliefs in necromancy.

In his writings, Northampton County historian

Matthew Henry told of witches who were seen with their arms locked together, dancing in a circles around a sturdy oak tree at the summit of Hexenkopf.

He wrote of unearthly sounds which emanated from the hill, and of ghostly lights which glowed on the ridge.

Charles E. Boyd, in his research on the history of Williams Township, claimed the reputed "powers" of Hexenkopf were first tapped by Dr. Peter Saylor, who practiced powwowing in the Raubsville area in the early part of the 19th century.

"While many exorcists used objects like a chair, an animal or, if handy, a corpse as receptors for the evils which they drew out from the patient under treatment, Dr. Saylor conceived the notion of using Hexenkopf as his gigantic receptor," Boyd reported.

It is said that Saylor tapped into the very bowels of the mountain for his power as he did much of his work in or near a cave near his home on the side of Hexenkopf.

A second-generation powwower, Saylor also apparently capitalized on the natural character of the hill when he cast his spell over those who came to partake of his talents.

Scattered deposits of mica on the rocks of Hexenkopf made it glitter in the moonlight. As Boyd said, "local people looked upon Hexenkopf as they would have looked upon the throne of the the Evil One Himself!"

Saylor passed on his "gift" to John H. Wilhelm, a neighbor, and the Wilhelm family continued the powwowing tradition of the Saylors. Local lore tells of crowds of buggies and people in tiny Raubsville as those hoping to partake of powwow healing assembled there.

One newspaper article claimed, "Many times at early dawn of the first Friday in the new moon, Raubsville was crowded with teams and vehicles of every description."

22

Powwowing gradually faded away in Raubsville, and the last known faith-healer who practiced in the grand Pennsylvania German tradition died in about 1950.

The powwowers and their patients in Williams Township were the central characters in a minor novel, "The Hex Woman," written by Earl Joseph ("Raube") Walters in 1931.

Much more serious documentation on whatever mysteries Hexenkopf holds is the evidence which indicates that a woman may actually have been taken to court after being charged with practicing witchcraft.

In a paper, "Hexenkopf: Mystery, Myth and Legend," Prof. Ned Heindel cited an 1863 article in a religious publication in which Rev. Charles P. Krauth recounted the legends of Hexenkopf, and further claimed that the witches "did not always escape with impunity."

Rev. Krauth quoted an court document in which jurors were given the case of a Williams Township, Northampton County widow who "did commit certain most wicked acts (called enchantments and charms)...maliciously and diabolically against a certain white horse."

The court paper, published with the names of the plaintiff and defendant and the exact dates omitted, noted that the accused, S_____ B_____, "at first resolutely denied the charge; but the learned judges at last convinced her of her guilt, and she always confessed herself a witch, though she was unable to say in what manner her enchantments had been performed."

The woman was punished with one year imprisonment and "every quarter to stand six hours in the pillory."

Dr. Heindel attempted to track down the court records at the Northampton County courthouse, but faced a disorganized, unindexed batch of 18th and 19th century transcripts and failed to locate the original paper.

23

Other stories of "hexerei" and the supernatural have circulated around Williams Township for generations.

A bedraggled old woman once wandered around the countryside, asking for sustenance at every farmhouse she reached. Believing she was a witch, the farmers obliged.

An old man had a vision of the ghost of his daughter, who told him to hasten to Hexenkopf, where he would find a fortune buried at a certain spot.

He followed the spirit's instructions, and after digging furiously at the prescribed location, he was frightened out of his boots by the booming voice of a massive figure in white which warned him to leave or face horrible consequences.

One story which involves Hexenkopf tells of the ghost of a peg-legged man which can be seen just after dusk on the hill. It is the spirit of a farmer who tumbled from the rocks to his death while pursuing a witch. This wraith, nicknamed "Farmer Brown," is said to have tousled, gray hair and a long beard. His ghost is easily recognizable by the eerie tapping of his wooden leg on the rocks.

An old folk tale around what some have called "Misery Mountain" also speaks of the ghosts of two farmers who, in life, engaged in a volatile dispute over a property line on Hexenkopf.

After both men passed on, their feud continued, taking the shape of terrible bolts of fire and a putrid stench which can be discerned from time to time on the hill.

A headless hunter and his companion, an equally decapitated dog, have been seen wandering on Hexenkopf, and an unearthly, elusive white fox has befuddled marksmen on the hill for decades.

While the stories of the hauntings of Hexenkopf have been diluted, and sometimes discredited by time,

24

there are those who live around "Misery Mountain" who will never discount its powers.

"I won't venture to the rocks at night, and positively not on Halloween," says Jane Knapp.

The woman lives on Hexenkopf Road, and her reason for avoiding any confrontations with the powers that may or may not be on the mountain stem from some very personal experiences.

"On Halloween, many years ago," she said, "Robert Seip, of New Jersey, asked his sister, Dorothy Knapp, if he could host a party at her home.

"Her house was more accommodating for a large group, and was located across the street from Hexenkopf Rock. During the course of the party, at midnight, Bob and a few of his friends wanted to walk over to the rock to add to the mystique of Halloween.

"The Halloween party took place, and at midnight, as planned, a few people went up to the rock. Not one of the local Williams Township natives even considered venturing to the rocks for fear of the witches."

Knapp was firm in her conviction regarding that mountain, and its witches. "It was like a superstition, but, it used to be that Witch Doctors would take evil spirits up to the rock and dump them off there, supposedly. If you irritate them, or make them angry, they get back at you."

She has reason to believe that claim.

Following their little jaunt to the haunted rock, all returned, and continued with their Halloween festivities.

"Several weeks later," Knapp continued, "many mishaps and tragedies followed. There was a thunder and lightning storm, and it knocked a tree down that missed a neighbor's home by a couple feet. That same neighbor, who lived in back of the house where the party was held, was working at a department store and one day when she was loading things on a shelf, things fell down and hit her, and she had to go to the hospital."

Another of the adventurers later suffered a hernia and needed treatment. Still another suffered the loss of his pet dog, which was struck by a car about a week after his master's Halloween hike on Hexenkopf.

Jane Knapp's personal recollections of the hill are enhanced by the lurid stories which have swirled around Williams Township for decades.

"There was a blind girl who climbed the rock," she recalled. "She had fallen down, and where she had fallen, you can see the outline of a witch's head on the rocks. A lot of people can see it, a certain way you look at it. It looks like the shape of the head of a witch."

She admitted that many people are still frightened of Hexenkopf, especially at night.

"Oh, yeah," she said, "they're superstitious. They respect the witches.

"One may say this is just a story," Jane affirmed, "but I will not venture to the rocks at night, and positively not on Halloween. I just hope the witches don't get upset for telling the story."

Near Reamstown, Lancaster County, is the place old timers called "es alt Hexefeld," or "the old witches' field."

A phenomenon known as "crop circles" swept the south of England in the 1980s and 1990s. Throughout wheat and corn fields in Sussex and parts of other English counties, odd and intricate patterns were matted into the fields. Some said they were caused by energy sources under the soil. Some said they were created by alien beings. Some said they were hoaxes.

These strange and unexplainable crop circles have nothing on good, old Pennsylvania Dutch Country lore. It seems this sort of thing has been happening hereabouts for many, many years.

It has been written that a man named Weaver owned the tract of farm land upon which "Hexefeld" was located.

He would regularly report incidents of rings in his fields where crops would not grow. They were in symmetrical patterns, and he blamed them on the witches who danced their rituals there.

Another time, Weaver told his neighbors that he ventured out to Hexefeld just after a snowfall and noticed that there was a circular pattern of small footprints in the snow.

There would be nothing particularly odd about that, if it were not for the fact that there were no prints leading to or from the circle. Weaver reasoned these, too, were the work of wandering wintry witches.

Just south of Hamburg, Berks County, is a ridge known to locals as "Witches' Hill." The old-timers thereabouts are more likely to call it by its name in the Pennsylvania German dialect, "Hexe Barrick" or "Hexe Danz" (witches' dance).

In olden days, it was said that horses refused to ascend to the top of Witches' Hill, balking or sometimes rearing up and throwing their riders because they were tormented by unseen forces.

Even to the present day, there are recurring stories of automobiles stopping mysteriously on the hill which, incidentally, is traversed by Witchcraft Road.

Legend has it that it is the place where the witches congregate–where they dance on freshly-planted crops, and where they cavort on Walpurgis Night.

Walpurgis Night is the night of April 30, the traditional time the witches, hags, ghosts and phantoms came out to torment the farmers and villagers of Bavaria, Bohemia and other sections of eastern Europe.

In turn, the mortals would mount symbolic and substantive defenses against the supernatural mayhem.

Bonfires would be ignited, whips cracked,pots and pans would be clanked, and noises of all sorts would be made to scare the witches away.

Thorns and brambles would be spread around the
27

farm yards and sweet herbs would be strung around doorways of the farm house in an effort to fend off those from the other world.

Walpurgis Night also played a role in some powwow practices.

If a farmer believed his cattle were bewitched, or "hexed," he was urged to take red garlic, thyme, fennel, asplenium, senega, horehound and artemisia and pulverize them. The resulting substance, known as "Deivel's Dreck," (Devil's Candy) would then be placed on fresh bread and fed to the cattle on Walpurgis Night. The cattle would no longer be possessed.

When the German immigrants settled in southeastern and southcentral Pennsylvania, they brought these eerie traditions with them.

They also imported the cures and remedies which have become a part of the folklore of the "Dutch Country."

Some of these cures are so ludicrous that they have become almost humorous.

Some less pleasant precautions were often taken in the name of superstitious precaution.

A curious spectacle at area farms many years ago would have been the carcasses of hawks and other large birds which were hung on the walls of barns. Somehow, these grotesque displays also kept the demons away.

It has also been documented that in Manheim, Lancaster County, there was a grisly belief that demons could be kept away from the furnaces of area glass blowers if live puppies were tossed into the blazing furnaces from time to time.

Although the common perceptions of hexerei and powwowing is that they dealt solely with illnesses and injuries, one form of mysticism was aimed at preventing fire.

The Ephrata Cloister was and is a marvelous cluster of wooden buildings occupied by a religious sect in the mid to late 18th century.

It is a state historical site, and well worth a visit. The story of the German mystic Conrad Beissel and his community is told in a fascinating tour.

It is interesting to note that although the structures are wooden, there have been few fires which have caused substantive damage.

That good fortune could be attributed to the work of the *Feuer Segen*, or exorcism of fire.

Another export from Germany, this procedure was carried out mostly by Jews and gypsies centuries ago.

Here as there, those individuals who knew the secrets of the exorcism were sought out to carry out the complicated ceremony which would serve to prevent fires.

The exorcism was based on the phases of the moon, Hebrew, Latin and/or German incantations, amulets, and one or more inscriptions and symbols.

In several folklore collections at museums and historical societies are copies of elaborate broadsides on which prayers, called Fire Charms, were printed. These, too, were considered to be helpful in the prevention of fire.

It is interesting to note that these superstitions and suppositions have not been limited to what was considered the frontier fringe of civilized Pennsylvania.

Indeed, from its very beginning, and at its place of beginning, the Keystone State has been a hotbed of the occult.

While places such as Salem, Massachusetts have gained infamy for their witches and witch hunts, there have been witchcraft trials carried out in Pennsylvania, as well.

In the Colonial Records of the Pennsylvania Provincial Council, Volume I, it is recorded that "two old women, Margaret Mattson and Yeshro Hendrickson," stood accused of witchcraft.

Mrs. Mattson, who lived with her husband on a

plantation along the Ridley Creek in Delaware County, had become known locally as "The Witch of Ridley Creek" and was accused of using illicit powers to influence those around her.

Because of her alleged transgressions, she was arrested and ordered to stand trial before William Penn, his attorney general, a petit jury of 12 and a grand jury of 21 members.

After testimony was provided, a not guilty plea was entered and the juries deliberated, the judge read the verdict. Mrs. Mattson was found "Guilty of having the common fame of a witch, but not guilty in manner and form as she stands endicted (sic)."

In 1693, a year after the notorious Salem Witch trials and executions, a man and his two sons in Chichester, Chester County, were accused by the Concord Monthly Meeting of Friends of dealing in astrology, clairvoiancy and necromancy–all of which were considered blasphemous by the Quakers and illegal by the provincial government.

The Quakers met with the accused, Robert Roman, and tried to persuade him to give up his evil ways. Several members of the congregation visited the man and his sons, but could not convince them that what they had been studying–and perhaps practicing–was wrong.

The matter eventually made its way into the courts. A Grand Inquest seized several books from the Roman house, and presented them to the judge as evidence that the men were involved in geomancy (a form of divining), necromancy and witchcraft.

After examining all evidence and hearing the defense, the judge handed down his final decision.

It was the order of the court that Roman "should pay five pounds for a fine and all the charges, and never practice the arts, but behave himself well for the future."

And so, from the earliest years of Pennsylvania's history to the moment you are reading this book, the powers of the supernatural have been a part of our society.

In this Pennsylvania "Dutch Country," mountains are named after hexes, roads are named after spooks and powwow doctors still hang their secret shingles in town and country.

Here, in artwork and literature, and in the fiber of folklore, the strange is accepted and the unexplained is commonplace.

‡

NETTIE MAY

Perhaps the most meaningful and interesting of all the tourist attractions of Lancaster County is the Landis Valley Museum, on Route 272, just north of Lancaster City.

Visitors may tour 18 buildings which span more than 200 years of farm and village life in this region of Pennsylvania.

From a blacksmith shop to a general store, a country hotel to a frontier farm yard, the open-air museum which is administered by the Pennsylvania Historical and Museum Commission, provides an educational and graphic glimpse into the lives, labors and leisure pursuits of those who helped develop the land known today as the Pennsylvania Dutch Country.

Special events and demonstrations are held at the museum during the year, and trained guides are available to interpret the buildings in the complex.

It is the *Landis Valley* Museum because it was the Landis family which sunk its roots into its soil in the early 18th century.

The Landis name can be traced to Switzerland as far back as 1438.

As the Anabaptist movement gained acceptance near Zurich, several Landis families formed a Mennonite congregation. Some members rose to become ministers in the faith, but because their beliefs conflicted with those of the prevailing society, they were silenced by imprisonment and/or execution.

32

In about 1660, several Landises moved into Germany to escape the religious persecution, but the arrests and executions continued.

In 1717, John, Jacob and Felix Landis decided to seek the freedom they cherished by sailing to the New World.

Jacob Landis landed in Philadelphia and worked his way inland to a place which now bears his name. Historians call him Pioneer Jake.

Several generations of Landises thrived in the rolling hills north of Lancaster for more than 200 years.

The direct line of descendants of Pioneer Jake Landis was broken in the mid 1950s when Henry and George Landis died. The museum concept, and many of its holdings, are their legacies.

Henry and George were born in 1865 and 1867, respectively. A younger sister, Anna, was born in 1862, but lived only five years.

And then, there was Nettie May.

Emma and Henry Landis gave birth to their last child in 1879, 18 years into their marriage and when Emma was 37 years old.

An eighth generation Landis, Nettie May was sickly from birth. Maybe because of that, and maybe because she was a surrogate for the deceased daughter, Nettie May became the classic "daddy's little girl."

Through diaries and the recollections of the last surviving Landis brothers, it was known that poppa Henry coddled and spoiled the lass.

Fate dealt Miss Landis a bad hand, however. In 1914, barely 34 years old, Nettie May departed this earth.

Or did she?

Dawn L. Fetter is a tour guide at the Landis Valley Museum. She has also become a student of the Landis family.

Born into a Pennsylvania Dutch family, Dawn learned much from her father, who was a well-respected

33

local folklorist.

During slack times at the museum, Dawn pores over the diaries left behind by Landis family members. She has reconstructed entire lives, events and households through these detailed documents.

"I feel I know these people personally," she said.

What's more, she feels one of them may still be with us–in a familiar place but an unfamiliar form.

One of the buildings on the museum tour is the splendid, Victorian Landis House.

It is the spiritual centerpiece of the museum–perhaps figuratively and literally.

Words roll from Dawn Fetter's lips in the distinctive "Dutchified" accent of the region.

J's become CH's, W's and V's exchange sounds, an OW becomes an AH, and words unfamiliar to the outsider sneak in from time to time.

It is a charming brogue delivered by a charming woman.

Dawn set the stage early and earnestly.

"I guess I do believe in ghosts," she asserted, because things have happened to me that I just can't figure out."

Naturally, Dawn's favorite stop when she gives tours is the Landis House. But, other guides have not necessarily shared Dawn's enthusiasm for the place.

"We did have a guide here, an elderly man, who would not go into the Landis House with tour groups, because he felt there were ghosts in it," she continued.

She added that there have been other guides who have refused or been reluctant to enter the house.

"Doors screech, footsteps have been heard there, and that type of thing," she said, matter-of-factly.

A popular story around the museum water cooler is of a former employee who was quietly going about her business on an upper floor of the Landis house when, with no human aid, the sweet sound of music began tinkling from a music box.

"That thing hadn't been wound, and hadn't played in years," Dawn chuckled. "It scared the heck out of the woman. She got out of the place as quickly as she could!

"And in the front room of the house, there's a curtain that's always falling down. The curator puts it up, and the curtain falls down. We don't know what causes that, either," she said.

Actually, Dawn–and others in the museum–have a very real feeling about what–and even *who*– may be causing the untoward episodes in the Landis House.

A confirmation of a sort came from a surprising and totally unexpected source.

"I was stationed in the Landis House several years ago," Dawn said. "I had quite a large group of people to give a tour to. I was telling them about the Landis family and how the two brothers founded the museum.

"All of a sudden, one of the women said 'there's a spirit in this house!'

"I really didn't know exactly how to handle it, because you have to be careful when you have other people. Well, I asked her, 'there is?' She said, 'yes, it is the spirit of a young girl.'

"Well, there's no way that these people, and that woman, could have known about the stories. They were from out of state. They would not have known the circumstances of the daughter as she fit in the family.

"She said it again. It's the spirit of a girl. She's a young girl and she died early in life.

"Then, she asked if she could pray for the spirit. Well, I told her that if she wanted to do that, she'd have to wait until the tour was finished.

"We went through the house with the tour, and the lady would not leave. She told me there was the ghost of a young girl who was very loved by her family. She told me about her personality, that she was sick from birth, and she told me things that people would not have

35

known."

The woman, who to this day is unidentified, also told Dawn that the spirit's name began with an "N."

As in Nettie.

"Then," Dawn concluded, "the woman got on her hands and knees and she prayed for the girl's spirit.

"When she was done, she told me not to worry, the spirit was at ease."

Actually, despite the unexplainable incidents and strange sounds experienced in the Landis House, Dawn has also felt at ease in the building.

"I really do feel comfortable there," she said through a contented grin. "I wish that if there was somebody or something in there, it would come out and talk to me. I'd have a whole lot of questions!"

The Landis Valley Museum is a lasting tribute to Henry and George Landis, who left no children to carry on their branch of the family's name.

The museum is their legacy.

Nettie May Landis likewise left no progeny. But, it could very well be that her legacy is her very spirit which dwells still today in the old family home.

‡

THE GHOST OF GYPSY HILL ROAD

It's hard to believe Terri Williams' description of what her "dream house" looked like before she and husband Steve purchased it in 1984.

"A dump," she called it. Run down after years of neglect, split into two apartment units and ravaged by vandals who took over when the previous tenants left, the stately brick home where Gypsy Hill Road meets Route 222 was the classic "handyman's special."

That, in essence, was what Steve could have been called–a true handyman.

After the Williamses purchased the old place that December, Steve and Terri put their talents together.

Using his experience in the roofing, siding, construction and landscaping trades, Steve went to work rebuilding everything inside and out of the three-feet thick walls of the 19th century, brick farmhouse.

They pumped several feet of rancid water out of the basement, chased the resident rats away, and brought in 200 tons of topsoil to remake the lawn.

Nothing escaped Steve and Terri's attention. They put a lot of effort into the restoration, but most of all they put a lot of love into it.

A privacy fence, a shrub-caressed brick walkway, a mature shade tree canopy and a cozy entrance nestled off Gypsy Hill Road belie the fact that the house faces the busy highway.

Farm fields frame the Williams property, which was

37

carved out of land once part of the Penn grant to Lancaster County pioneer Hans Herr.

Adding its own particular kind of character to the property is a small family graveyard which is set just past the Williams property line.

Tombstones in the old Lefever family plot date from 1714 to 1799. It is still visited often by family members, according to Terri Williams.

The Williams family is justifiably proud of its home, and Terri said there just might be someone or something else in the place who shares their pride.

It's not the rats–they're long gone. But it could be the cats.

"That's what Steve says," quipped Terri. "Every time something does happen, Steve blames it on Annie or Raisin. I don't know, maybe they could have done some of the things, but other things that happened couldn't have been done by the cats."

Steve is fairly blasé about the notion of ghosts. His only profound experience was when he and Terri were watching television and a video camera placed on a table in an adjoining room clicked and whirred.

He looked over in amazement as what he later described as a blurry, gray object seemed to materialize and wend its way toward the camera.

He got Terri's attention, asked her if she saw what he saw, and got a negative response.

Steve went to check on the camcorder, specifically to see if anything unusual was recorded on it. Nothing was, and in fact the lens cap was on.

"I've always been a believer that there's another dimension out there somewhere," said Terri, a graduate of Garden Spot High School. "And," she continued, "in a house this old, something's bound to happen."

Terri and Steve have done research on their homestead. They discovered that a building stood on the site in an 1864 map, and that their particular house was built in 1888.

"I often think that in a house that's been around this long, there's been a lot of human drama. I would suppose people have died in here," Terri said.

"We did find out that someone was killed right out front in an automobile accident," she added. An intelligent and rational person, Terri was not quick to associate that fact with the unexplained activities which have played out in their home.

Most of the episodes have been relatively insignificant and inoccuous. Still, they have left Terri with the gut feeling that Raisin and Annie are innocent as charged by Steve and something a bit more unworldy may be taking place.

"We were in there less than a year," she related, "and we had two beautiful azaleas out front. My father-in-law gave them to us from his church, and we planted them that spring. They were in full bloom and very beautiful.

"Well, we happened to drive past the front of the house just after we had planted them and one of the plants was missing.

"I thought, now who could do that? Who would rip out a beautiful azalea plant?

"Then, I looked closer to where we had planted it. It was as if no plant had ever been planted there. The soil appeared to be undisturbed, the mulch was untouched, and it was if no hole was ever dug, no plant ever planted...it was strange."

One of the peccadilloes of the old farmhouse is that the door which leads from the master bedroom into the attic has a habit of sticking.

If for no other reason, Terri doesn't mind because she knows that once the door is pulled shut, it *stays* shut.

That's why she was more than a little miffed when she and Steve returned home from a vacation trip one time to find the attic door swung wide open. She knew—she had double-checked before they left—that the door had been pulled shut and, as it was wont to do, was stuck.

There had been caretakers at the house in their absence. None reported any intrusions, none had gone anywhere near the attic door.

Another time, a decorative folk art heart which was securely mounted high above a kitchen door fell to the floor without any known assistance. And on still another occasion, several inches of weatherstripping around a door from the recreation room to the basement was peeled back.

While not particularly "ghostly" in nature, the incidents gave the family pause for thought.

When Terri related those occurrences to a friend, that superstitious friend pointed out to her that each thing had taken place on or around a door which leads out of the main living area.

Perhaps, that friend thought, if there was a ghost in the place, it was sending Terri and Steve some sort of message.

Another incident involving a door is the most confounding.

Terri had occasion to go into the basement one time, and as she had done many times before, she opened the door which led downstairs.

She did a double-take when the door wobbled and came off one of its hinges.

Having become intimate with the house, the restoration of it, and its "personality," Terri immediately thought the pin in the upper hinge had somehow worked its way out. She would find the pin elevated beyond the point it could hold the door, or perhaps altogether off and on the floor.

She looked at the hinge. The pin was in place, perfectly and securely in place. The door's half of the hinge was unbroken and seemingly untouched!

Terri's fascination and affection for the old place has led to a certain amount of admitted flights of fantasy about the house.

Upstairs, there's a room, built into the middle of the attic. "It's a weird room," Terri said. "When we moved in, it was padlocked, like they used to keep somebody up there!"

She since has been told that such a room in such a house may well have been the smoking room, in which the farm family smoked its meats.

"Well, I guess so," Terri deferred, "but it's still a strange little room."

Nothing destructive has ever happened to the Williamses as the result of any unexplained activity in their house. There have been some rather baffling nights, though.

"It was really hot one night a few summers ago," she related, "and we were in bed with the window open.

"It was about 2:30 in the morning, and I woke up to the sound of some kind of music filtering in from somewhere out there. I listened closely. It was so faint that I had to hold my breath to hear it. But there it was. It was some kind of calliope music, or the kind of parlor music they played back in the last century. It was definitely there.

"Even Steve heard it. And, we checked the next day to see if there was any kind of fair or carnival nearby that night. There wasn't."

Terri is not afraid of the house, or anything which may be in that "other dimension" she believes is very real. "I've always felt safe and comfortable here," she said.

It may be that Terri Williams has a subliminal desire to meet whoever may be wandering invisibly in their midst.

She related an eerie experience which may lie at the very foundation of what she may discover–should she

41

seek a psychic interpretation.

"I kept having a recurring dream about a mysterious woman in a blue dress," she admitted. "She was somewhere around me, in that house.

"For about six months, I would sometimes sit up in bed and wait for her to wander down the hall and maybe into the room."

Was Terri's dream a harbinger of something to come? Is there a ghost in the Williams house on Gypsy Hill Road?

Could it be the spirit of someone who passed away in the house? The traffic fatality victim? The restless wraith of someone buried in the little graveyard just beyond their property line?

Perhaps one day Terri and Steve will find out for certain.

‡

THE ETERNAL HUNTER

There are few forested mountain slopes in Lancaster County.

In what is left of the those wooded hills, however, many strange and haunting legends abound. One is an enduring phantom who is more often heard than seen, and who makes his presence known most vividly in the dead of winter.

In the Pennsylvania Dutch dialect, he is called "die Eewich (or Ewige)Yeager (or Jaeger)." Either way, it translates to "The Eternal Hunter."

To those who take to the forests and fields in the hills and valleys in the Dutch Country, it is a legend which has prevailed since the first nimrod took musket to muskrat, and at times it is all to real.

Just who the Eternal Hunter may be is a matter of speculation. The premise itself can be found in the folklore of countless peoples and regions.

In the Pennsylvania Dutch Country, however, the story is most often traced to the fires of the Cornwall Furnace in Lebanon County.

It has been told best in the epic poem, "The Legend of the Hounds," by George H. Boker.

Boker was a prominent Pennsylvania poet, and his work which details the origins of the Eternal Hunter is of the quality of Edgar Allan Poe. Excerpts of it will weave throughout this telling of the tale.

It is generally accepted by historians that most of the masters of the many iron plantations in southeastern

Pennsylvania in the 18th and 19th centuries were benevolent types who treated those in their charge with as much dignity and respect as the times and tasks would allow.

These plantations were more like self-sufficient villages. The Cornwall Furnace, a state historic site, and Hopewell Furnace, a national historic site, are prime examples of these massive operations. Both are open for public visitation.

The blast furnace itself was the centerpiece of a complex which included farm fields, clusters of workers' homes, a company store, tradesmens' shops, and the ironmaster's mansion.

From these plantations came products which ranged from cannon and cannon balls for Washington's army to stoves for the early American consumer.

Cornwall Furnace produced pig iron from 1742 to 1883, and iron ore was still taken from mines around the furnace until the 1970s.

Colebrook Furnace in Cornwall stands,
Crouched at the foot of the iron lands,
The wondrous hill of iron ore
That pours its wealth through the furnace door,
Is mixed with lime and smothered in wood,
Tortured with fire till a molten flood
Leaps from the taps to the sow below
And her littered pigs that 'round her glow;
So that a gazer looking down
The moulding floor from the platform's crown,
Might think, if fancy helped the spell,
He saw a grate in the roof of hell!

The story is told about an ironmaster at Cornwall who was inordinately cruel to those who worked for him. He ruled his dismal domain with dictatorial power, and was at once feared, despised and respected by those who stoked and sustained the fires of the furnace.

The ironmaster was also reputed to be somewhat of a lout, often distracted by whiskey, women and the lure of the fox hunt.

Strong of sinew and dull of mind,
He blustered around like a winter wind.
You could hear his laugh come on before
While his hounds were off a mile or more;
And in the wassail he stormed and roared,
Clashing his fist on the groaning board,
Or clutched his trulls till their young bones bent,
And they shrieked at his savage merriment.

This tyrant drew no bounds with his contempt. He treated his many mistresses as he treated his workers.

What's more, his disdain for any modicum of dignity extended into the pack of hounds which led his many hunts.

These canine servants came and were discarded at the ironmaster's whim. One, and in Boker's poem it was named Flora, somehow withstood the master's wrath and was "top dog" for many years.

Flora, the leader of his pack,
Followed, a shadow in his track;
Followed despite his kicks and blows,
Paused when he paused, rose when he rose.
Nestled beneath his clumsy feet
When all the table swam with heat,
And causeless oath and witless joke
Around the swinish circle broke;
And sometimes when her drunken lord
Slid stupefied beneath the board,
And stouter comrades jeered his plight
With pointed thumbs and laughter light,
She howled above the Squire's disgrace,
Or, moaning, licked his flaming face.

Faithful or foolish, Flora was spared the ironmaster's fury simply because she was unmatched at the head of the pack as it took out after its prey in the fields around Cornwall.

In field no hound could hold the scent
With Flora, as she bounding went.
Ten lengths before the yelping chase,
And kept throughout her leading place.
Unchallenged in the flying front,
She shone, a star, to all the hunt.

Flora was more than the lead hound in the hunt. She was his constant companion, despite all the abuse she was forced to endure.

One stormy winter's night, after the ironmaster had collapsed unconscious in a drunken coma in the thick snow, Flora aroused him by barking until he came to.

She lapped her warm tongue on his face to soften his freezing features and led him to warmth and safety.

With all the vigor of her strength,
Dragged him along, good half a rood;
And fairly on his feet she stood
The man, bewildered and half dead,
He staggered forward where she led.

One beautiful autumn day, the ironmaster invited several influential individuals to a day of hunting. He had bragged about his fine hounds and the fertile fields which would provide many a handsome trophy.

Over hill and across creek they went. It was to be a day of exciting challenges and a night of revelry and reflection on the many pelts which would be collected.

Instead, the ironmaster's pack was lethargic and lackluster.

For all his boasts, the squire's fine pack
Sulked at the outset, and held back,
With dropping tail and humble head,
And deprecating eyes that said,

Almost as tongues, this morning's sport
Finds us with spirits slack and short.

Infuriated, the ironmaster demanded the dogs impress his guests. They were whipped incessantly. They were damned, they were punished and cursed, and they still would not perform.

Those who he had hoped to impress were soon mocking and tormenting the ironmaster and his listless legion.

His whip and temper both blazing, the ironmaster turned his pack and party toward his "big house."

It was a savage ride. No dog was spared his wrath.

Amid the cowering dogs he dashed,
Rode over some, cursed all, and lashed
Even Flora until her milky side
With trickling crimson welts was dyed.

The ironmaster's fury would subside, both dogs and riders hoped.

He would put an end to the embarrassing hunt and, his guests reckoned, drown his disgrace in a flood of whiskey back at the mansion.

The village was just over a rise. Smoke billowed from the furnace. The early evening sky was brilliant as the sunset and the fiery glow from the distant flames engaged in a skyborne scarlet duel.

There came a fork in the well-worn hunt trail. One path led to the master's mansion. The other led to the grim row of workers' houses and the furnace tunnel head.

As all drew wide-eyed with dread confusion, the master drove the dogs toward the furnace. It was simply not the way, nor where, one would end a hunt.

One of the hunters dared to inquire as to where the ironmaster was leading.

47

"Where? Why to Cornwall, down the glen—
I'll show these town bred gentlemen
If my dogs cannot hunt so well
On earth, another hunt in hell!"
Bowled the mad Squire; and all the beast
In his base nature so increased;
That he could crown the deed he sought
With laughter brutal as the thought.

With sinister glee, the master shrieked and thrashed until the group reached the furnace.

Beside the furnace, wondering still
What freak the angry Squire might will,
The hunt dismounted. "Up!" he said,
"Up with you, to the furnace head!
Yes, bring the dogs." The whips looked blank.
Some muttered, "Nonsense!" and some shrank
From the fierce heat that overran
The reeking walls. "Up, dog and man!"
Yelled forth the Squire, "By Heav'n you'll rue,
If any balk the thing I'd do!

With that, the cruel master stunned the firemen, the huntsmen, and curious onlookers with a harsh demand. A hush fell over the gathering.

"Come here, you drones, and work a spell!
Look at your furnace! Can you tell
What needs a fire so dull and slack?
Feed it, you sluggards, with this pack!"

The crowd murmured. The firemen protested. Theirs, however was not to reason.

Into the flames with howl and yell,
Hurled by the rugged firemen, fell
That pack of forty. Better hounds,
Fuller of music, of the sounds,
That fire the hunter, drawing near
His furry prey with whoop and cheer—

48

The dogs all bursting in full cry,
Crashing through brush and timber high—
Never could Cornwall boast; and still
The silent lands lamented their ill,
And the mysterious spell that lay
Upon them on that fatal day.
For now the bubbling, liquid fire
Swallowed them all. Beside the Squire,
Flora alone stood desolate,
Sole relique of the general fate.

The lurid deed was done. Forty fine hounds, smitten by languor that day, were cast into the fire. Only Flora was spared.

The master gazed into the pyre. Slowly, he turned to face those who stood in silence after watching his crazed order carried out to the fullest.

Eyes reflecting red from the flames, he fixed a stare on faithful Flora.

As if she shared the shock and foretold her fate, she bared her fangs and growled. The growl became a roar, and the roar a deafening "AARGH" which rose above the crackling of the furnace fire.

The Squire was shaken from his stupor by Flora's bloodcurdling yowl.

He looked Flora square in the eyes which once gave him comfort and solace. He became a tornado of emotions.

"You shrinking cowards," foamed the Squire,
Now with redoubled rage afire,
"Is it for your pretty skins you fear
To venture? Flora—here, dog—here!"
At once the look of wrath was gone;
A trusting, tender, loving dawn
Rose in her eyes; a low soft wail
Broke from her as the iron hand
Of the stout Squire from off her stand
Swung her; and striding towards the ledge
With his pleased burden, on the edge

49

Of awful death–oh, foul disgrace!
She turned and licked his purple face.
Sheer out he flung her, as she fell,
Up from that palpitating hell
Came three shrill cries, and then a roll
Of thunder. Every pallid soul
Shrank away from the pit; and ghastly white,
As was the snow one winter night.
The Squire reeled backward. Long he gazed
From face to face; then asked, amazed,
"Was it a fancy? If you heard,
Answer! What was it?–that last word
Which Flora flung me?" Answer came,
As though one mouth pronounced the name,
And smote the asker as a rod;
"The word she said was –'God, God, God!'"

A horrified look swept the ironmaster's face. All had confirmed what he believed he had heard. As the flames were consuming dear Flora, the dying dog gasped one last plea for mercy.

Overcome with grief when he finally realized what he had done, the ironmaster retired to his mansion. Those who had watched him carry out the canine carnage walked silently into the night.

Back in his room, alone, the ironmaster stared into the eternity to which his hounds had been cast. After a few hours, he passed out, poisoned by the whiskey he had hoped would only numb his maniacal senses.

He would never hunt again–in life. For days, and then weeks, and then months, he would sit disconsolate in his bed. His eyes were affixed in a deathly glare. He clasped tightly his whip. His life was slowly, painfully draining from his body.

His servants and staff maintained a vigil. Their Squire's face grew ever pallid, his eyes ever hollow. Nary a smile nor emotion of any kind disturbed his face.

He was left to pass his days in agony.

And then, as all were settling in for another

eventless evening in the mansion, the master's voice rattled within the walls.

> *Shouting, so all the house might hear,*
> *Aghast with more than mortal fear,*
> *"Here they all come, the hellish pack,*
> *Pouring from Cornwall Furnace, back*
> *Into the world! Oh, see, see, see!*
> *They snuff, to get the wind of me!*
> *They've found it! Flora heads the whole—*
> *Whiter than any snows that roll*
> *Now they give tongue! They've found their prey!*
> *Here they come crashing, all this way—*
> *And all afire! And it is I...*
> *Weak as I am, and like to die—*
> *Who must be hunted!" With a bound*
> *He reached the floor, and fled around.*
> *Once, twice, thrice, round the room he fled,*
> *Then in the nurses' arms fell dead.*

The ghostly hounds had exacted their revenge. The ironmaster died, eyes wide open in a death stare.

At that moment, The Legend of the Hounds was born. As George H. Boker concluded his poem.

> *Still Cornwall Furnace grimly stands,*
> *Waving its plume o'er Cornwall's lands,*
> *Blighting the air with poisoned breath,*
> *Spreading the bounds of waste and death,*
> *Its slag and cinder, dry and dun,*
> *That nothing green will grow upon;*
> *Still like a hoary king, it rears*
> *Its head among its dismal peers;*
> *Still at its glowing feet are rolled*
> *The floods that turn to wicked gold;*
> *Still beasts, birds, reptiles shun the place;*
> *And the man alone will do it grace;*
> *The Squire and all his race are gone,*
> *But this wild legend still lives on.*
> *Christ save us from the wretched fate*
> *Of him who dared his wrath to sate*
> *On God's dumb creatures, as of old*

Befell the Squire of whom I told!

According to historian Dr. Herbert H. Beck, Boker's work so disturbed the surviving family of the ironmaster who was suspected of being the perpetrator of the evil act that they bought up all but three copies of the first edition of Boker's poem and destroyed them.

The copy used for this adaptation was obtained from the U.S. National Park Service.

Dr. Beck examined the Eewich Yeager story and discovered a version in which the lead dog's name was "Singing Ann," and the ironmaster became unsuccessfully repentant in his last earthly gasps.

He even placed the time of the ironmaster's death (March, 1790), and involved an individual whose own legend lives on as a geographical nameplace in southern Lebanon County.

Near Cornwall and Mt. Gretna is a hill which bears the unusual name of Governor Dick Mountain.

It is named after a Cornwall Furnace slave and collier who lived in a crude cabin at the foot of the hill. He had spent his childhood with a master along Currituck Sound, North Carolina, but lived out the rest of his life burning charcoal at Cornwall.

It was Governor Dick who figured in the legend of the old ironmaster. It was he who was by the side of the Squire when death claimed him.

It was he who heard the final utterances of the ironmaster, and he who spread the word throughout Cornwall that the man who drove the dogs to death was himself dead.

According to Governor Dick, through Dr. Beck's interpretation, the ironmaster's deathbed torpor was broken with him exclaiming, "Why did I do it? Why? Why? Why? Why did I order my huntsman to drive my pack of foxhounds into the blazing top of my blast furnace? Why didn't I give them another chance?

Another day they might have worked better.

"They could always drive their fox before. Why should they have failed me on that one day; to the disgust and ridicule of my drunken Philadelphia friends?

"And that my favorite hound, Singing Ann, had to go into that hot hell with the rest! Why? Why?! So help me God. Come back...come back! Singing Ann, come back!"

Those were the ironmaster's final words. As he implored his favorite hound to return from the dead, he himself was taken by the Grim Reaper.

Out in the nearby woods, a Hessian slave and huntsman who had trained the dead pack of hounds, suddenly was distracted and looked into and through the spiny winter tree branches.

Somewhere, in the void of darkness which enveloped the nightscape, the soft baying of hounds could be heard.

The barking grew louder, closer.

It was a familiar sound to the Hessian. But tonight, the clamor came as if from the firmament, not the fields.

As he cocked an ear to listen to the unwordly sound, Governor Dick scurried by, alerting him to the fact that the ironmaster had just passed away.

The Hessian stood rigid and frozen in fear.

"Verdammmpt sei!," he exclaimed, "Es ist der Ewige Jaeger!"

He knew all to well that as the last embers of life within the ironmaster grew cold, his spirit found new fire, doomed to follow his phantom foxhounds forever in the sky of eternal darkness.

To this day, the sound of yelping hounds, the roar of horses' hooves and the muffled commands of the crazed ironmaster can still be heard in the forests of the Pennsylvania Dutch Country highlands.

✣

THE GHOST IN THE GARDEN

There are few towns along the Susquehanna River with the charm and quaint elegance of Marietta.

Off the main highways and snuggled against the broad river, Marietta's Market Square is quaint and tidy, and there are several fine restaurants, shops and bed and breakfast inns in and around the town.

Most of what helped build Marietta has passed on, passed by, or rushes through the town these days.

Most of the old factories are shuttered. The state highway zooms along to the east. The river carries no traffic, the canal has gone dry, and railroad service is a memory.

But the people of Marietta have not forgotten their town's proud past. Many houses have been beautifully restored and periodic special events pay tribute to the history and heritage of the handsome home of some 3,000 residents.

David Cook and James Anderson had laid out towns which were situated next to one another. In 1810, they agreed to combine their developments into one, more sizable community. For the name of the new town, they chose also to combine and contract the names of their wives, *Mary* and Henr*ietta.*

In the early 1820s, as commerce on the river and the new canal grew busier, there was a need for a place where those who worked the waterways could find food, drink and rest. Enterprising businessmen erected a hotel of sizable proportions directly along the Pennsylvania Main

Line Canal.

"It's walls reverberated with inebriate good cheer, an occasional brawl, and all the violence and immorality of the roughest classes," is the way one contemporary account described life in what was called the "Railroad House."

As the canal prospered, so did the hotel. And, as the railroad replaced the canal in the mid-19th century, the hotel's fortunes shifted from barges and locks to boxcars and tracks.

The hotel became Marietta's railroad station, as the ticketing office and waiting room were situated in the building until the Marietta Station was built across the street in 1860.

Legends abound up on the north end of town of how ladies of questionable repute would sit provocatively on the front porch of the hotel and tempt railroad workers as they went about their business.

The hotel operation survived until the Great Depression and a 1936 flood of the Susquehanna sapped the life from it.

Sold at public auction in the 1950s, the building survived the 1960s, serving as, among other things, a psychedelic coffee house.

In 1972, another great flood washed away the checkered past, and the hotel was reborn as a gourmet restaurant and night club.

When Donna and Rick Chambers considered purchasing the old place at Front and Perry Streets, they saw behind its aging facade a fine Victorian structure which would serve well as a fine dining spot and a cozy bed and breakfast.

That's exactly what the Chambers created as they pumped new life into the Railroad House.

But, it's quite possible that there's an old life that still remains in a supernatural limbo just beyond the walls of the restaurant/inn.

Rick and Donna are fiercely and justifiably proud of their property. A main dining room, decorated in the "Music Room" theme which gave it its name, was the old railroad waiting room.

What was the original kitchen is now the "Country Room," and the basement is the "Arrivals Tavern." Twelve rooms, upstairs and in the old summer kitchen, are guest rooms, and a back patio and garden accommodates *alfresco* functions in season.

It is in that stately English Garden, just beyond the patio, where the ghost they call Anna Marie has been seen.

She's been seen by several employees, and is well known to neighbors.

"I didn't think much of it," said Rick Chambers, "but then I heard some other people talk about her...people who knew her."

Those folks included a bartender at the nearby Shank's Tavern, and other people who have spent many years along Front Street.

"From what I was told," Chambers continued, "she lived next door. She lived there for a number of years up to about the turn of the century."

Piecing together shards of information gleaned from several sources, Rick and Donna have determined the woman who was named Anna Marie and the ghostly image which has been seen in the garden are one and the same.

That garden is fashioned in the classic English style. Flower, vegetable and herb plantings are highlighted by the presence of such "personality" trees as a so-called Walking Cane Tree and a Weeping Cherry.

Weddings are performed in the gazebo, and herbs used as garnish or ingredients in some of the restaurant's menu offerings are actually grown in the pleasant setting.

"When people go out to pick mint," Donna said, "they sometimes see her. She just seems to come out, mostly at night, and work on her own vegetable garden."

Donna added that while she has never seen Anna Marie herself, she has felt a kind of comforting feeling in the Railroad House that she was never really alone.

Rick said a former Railroad House chef swore he saw the faint but identifiable form of a woman, bent over in the garden.

"He, and another former employee told me that they both saw her out there, picking flowers. Once she saw them, she just disappeared," he noted.

From what Rick and Donna have learned from neighbors, Anna Marie took pride in her garden. In her day, the land on which the present plot is laid out was considered to be shared property between the hotel and its next-door neighbor.

Although the legal property lines may have been redrawn, the ghostly Anna Marie recognizes no such bounds.

There are 12 bedrooms in the portion of the Railroad House which is the "bed" of "bed and breakfast." One of them, Room Six, may also harbor an unseen presence.

"We have also heard recently, that there is a ghost in our attic," Donna confirmed. "All we know is that somebody supposedly shot themself in one of the rooms. We have heard it was in room six, but we don't know much more about it."

Donna does recall, however, an odd incident which took place when the Chambers were moving into the old hotel.

"When we first came here," she remembered, "I was up in room number six, by myself, in the dark, changing my shoes or something. I thought I heard the sounds of muffled musket gunshots. I even told Rick about it. It was strange."

Also in the moving-in process, another unexplainable incident played out.

"We found two mysterious little leather or suede pouches upstairs. They had, well, some substance which could have been ashes in them. It made me wonder, because we bought the place from the estate of someone who had died and had been cremated. Well, you never know," she said, her voice trailing away in thought.

Both Rick and Donna, and certain employees, have heard the sound of footsteps where no feet were stepping, and some folks have reported hearing other unaccountable sounds.

An employee, Tonia Archer, once spent a night there with her cousin, Sherry Quay. They were the only people in the place that night, and both claim to have heard the very clear sound of typing coming from an adjoining room–where there was no typewriter.

There is no fear or discomfort on the part of the Chambers or any individual who has heard the sounds or seen the apparition of Anna Marie.

"If there's a ghost in here," Donna said with confidence, "it's harmless."

✢

THE GLOWING TRACTOR

"*I*'ll tell you my story on a few conditions. You don't use my name and you don't say exactly where this happened.

"You can say I was a cop, but nothing more."

And, since the man is a *big* cop, a no-nonsense kind of guy, we agreed to his conditions.

It is the bane of a ghost story collector and re-teller that anonymity be granted in many cases.

It does seem to chip away at the credibility factor, but agreeing to change names, dates and places is often the difference between securing and losing the story.

This will not be the only story in this book in which actual names are changed, and whenever they are, the reader will be advised.

In this case, let us call the man "the Chief" and say only that he is a retired police officer in a populous Lancaster County borough.

"I want you to know," he started, "I don't scare easily. I saw a lot of front line action during World War II and got involved in some pretty nasty things on the police force. But I'll tell you, this incident still raises the hair on my arms.

"It happened several years ago, but I still think about it often. I even avoid going to the area it took place in. My wife used to laugh about it but she's gotten used to it."

The Chief's words exploded from his robust face. His is a rumpled, character actor kind of face. He sneers.

59

He growls. His words are to be believed.

"I remember the night as if it was last week," the Chief continued as he pieced together the events of that Wednesday evening in the meticulous manner of a criminal investigator.

His seniority on the police force ensured him of steady day work, but that night, he was filling in for a fellow officer whose wife had gone into labor late in the afternoon. "It was a while since I had been in the cruiser," he laughed, "and even a lot longer since I was on the overnight shift.

"Nights in this area are pretty quiet. Weekends, you might have a few rowdies when the bar closes, or maybe a neighbor playing a stereo a little too loud. During the week, mostly traffic violations are what keep you busy.

"I don't know what time it was, sometime between one and two in the morning. Anyway, toward the southeast edge of town there was a bright light.

"I'm not ordinarily out at 1:30 a.m. to say this was unusual, but I know my area, and I know there was nothing over there that could or should cause that much light. Traffic was unusually heavy for some reason, so I decided to stay in town rather than go investigate whatever it was.

"Well, it was at least an hour before things got real quiet. I waited maybe another half hour, so that would be around three o'clock. The light was still there, so I decided to see what it was."

With that, the Chief paused and gathered his thoughts. It was obvious that whatever was about to spring from his lips would move him greatly.

"There's this small hill just out of town. I thought that when I got to the top of it I would see what was causing the light. When I got there, I was surprised to see that it was over the next rise, a couple miles farther south.

"To get to that spot, I had to drive through a small

wooded area, make a right hand turn, into what is mostly farm land.

"So finally I got to a field, and all it was was a farmer plowing his field. What really impressed me was the amount of light radiating from the tractor.

"The light wasn't just in front, as with headlights, but rather all around it, glowing. Something new, I figured.

"Actually, it didn't seem like a bad idea. A farmer plowing his fields at three in the morning isn't something you see that often, but some guys do work late when they have to.

"The tractor had just made its turn before I got there, and he was now moving away from me. I recognized the tractor immediately. It was an old John Deere that, well, call him 'Jake Meyers' used. I didn't get a look at the driver, but if it was Jake, it would all make sense.

"He used to say that he loved to farm, and I think he just worked to keep busy after his wife had died. Some people used to say he was working himself to death so he could join her up there earlier.

"I stood by the edge of the field until the tractor turned around and started to head back toward me. The light from the tractor was so bright that I started to walk into the field. It was like daytime!

"I walked about ten yards into the field before I knew for sure that it was Jake.

"What I saw next is something I'll never forget for the rest of my life. There was terror on this man's face such as I have never seen before. Now, I don't like to keep talking about the war days, but sometimes that's the only experience you can relate to. Right before battle, everyone is scared and it shows. But, it isn't until after the battle when the terror shows on the faces.

"The look on Jake's face, the look in his eyes, was more intense than anything I ever say on any faces in

Europe. I don't know how long we looked at each other, but it seemed like an eternity.

"Then, he was gone!"

A pregnant pause punctuated the story. The Chief drew a deep breath and cast his eyes toward the ceiling.

"Gone. Puff. Disappeared. Like in a magic act," he said in a voice which had started to quiver.

The best—or for the Chief, the worst—was yet to be said.

"Then, it wasn't just Jake," he said, expecting an incredulous retort, "it was the whole tractor, too!"

The Chief shuffled in his chair, folding and fumbling with his fingers.

"Now here I am," he continued, "a trustee of the public's well being, three o'clock in the morning, standing twenty yards into a field, wondering what the hell was going on.

"I know this all sounds strange, but here's the kicker—Jake had been dead for about three years when this all happened.

"Three years, this man is in his grave, and I see him plowing his field in the middle of the morning! I don't know how many times I fell or stumbled getting out of that field. I don't know how long I sat in that squad car, either.

"As a matter of a fact, the rest of that morning is a blank to me, even to this day. The next thing I remember is my wife coming home and waking me the next day. She said she would start lunch while I was showering.

"I decided not to tell her, or anybody else, what happened. But, I knew I was only kidding myself. I have never been able to keep a secret from my wife.

"By the time I sat down at the kitchen table she was asking me what was wrong, I told her. Reluctantly, but I told her.

"We finished lunch and a couple pots of coffee and we were still discussing what had happened.

62

"It was my imagination, we decided. It wasn't a satisfactory answer, it didn't answer any questions, but it was an answer I could learn to live with. It was my imagination.

"But, I knew it wasn't.

"About one o'clock, the phone rang. It was for me. It was Mike down at the police station.

"He said he hated to call me at home, but said the office was swamped that morning with people saying they saw a bright light outside of town overnight. He asked if I had seen it and knew what it was.

"I told him it was my imagination.

"'Your what?,' he asked me.

"I caught myself. 'Uh, oh,' I told him, it was probably their imagination, I said. I don't know, Mike, I didn't see anything at all.

"Nothing at all."

The Chief looked away from the interviewer. There was nothing more for either to say.

‡

ADAMSTOWN APPARITIONS

The area around Adamstown is rich with one of the largest concentrations of antique and collectible dealers and flea markets in the United States.

The little town which straddles the Berks and Lancaster County border is also rich with fascinating legends which are peppered with the likes of ghostly women who walk the town's streets, a phantom dog and...headless pigs.

Yes, Sleepy Hollow along the Hudson has its headless horseman, but Adamstown along the Muddy Creek has its headless pigs.

Side-by-side many years ago in town were a butcher shop and the Echtenach distillery. It was said the grain residue from the distillery was graciously dumped over its fence and into the barnyard where the butcher fattened his swine.

The constant supply of choice grain made the hogs grow heavier and provided the butcher with a handsome business.

The story goes that so many hogs were butchered at the Adamstown abattoir that several residents reported seeing the headless ghosts of the beasts wandering aimlessly on the streets of town.

One of the most baffling and frightening ghost stories in Adamstown was and is the tale of two women, one clad in white and the other in black. They are, in the dialect, "die weiss fraa un die schwatz fraa."

These two spirits have been seen on various

occasions and by various people, at various places in town.

Some accounts said the two ghosts would never look at one another, or anyone they passed. They were never far from one another, and they could be seen at any time, any place.

Should any mortal follow them, however, they would always lead them toward a cemetery at the edge of town. There, they would pause a few moments, turn, and walk into the graveyard.

Once inside the cemetery, they would fade away and disappear.

Another spirit which has captured the imaginations of Adamstonians for generations is a small black dog of undetermined breed.

Simply, the dog has been known to materialize on a street, in a backyard, or actually in a home or business, linger a while, and vanish into thin air.

Adamstown is at the edge of the gently rolling hills which stretch northward to Galen Hall, South Mountain, and regions which are ripe with tales of the supernatural.

On one of the hills just outside of Adamstown is a land form which is on some old maps and in many old-timers' memories as the Devil's Race Track.

Many, many years ago, a German immigrant kept a humble cabin in the woods near the "race track." He would often come into town and to rural churches, grange halls, fire companies and the like and entertain with his fiddling.

He was well known at weddings, local carnivals and other events, and he kept whatever monetary payments he would receive in a small box in his cabin. It was believed he saved the money to eventually have enough to bring his mother over from "the old country."

He also maintained a job as a farm hand, but the wages earned there went to the church and little bags of candy he would hand out readily to children he would meet.

Tradition has it that it was an October 24 in a year of the early 19th century when the fiddler was accosted in his cabin.

It was around midnight. The gent had just returned from a local fiddling "gig," and he was horrified to find a pair of thugs waiting for him inside his front door.

The two intruders demanded his money. The fiddler stood his ground, refusing to lead them to his secret stash.

The robbers became murderers as they savagely beat the fiddler. After the grisly deed was done, they tore the cabin apart looking for any money which could be found. They found none, and in frustration they took a torch to the log walls and burned the place to the ground.

To this day, folks who find their way to the Devil's Race Track report hearing the eerie sound of violin music echoing through the woods.

Especially tempting to a prospective ghost hunter is the prospect that when the clock strikes midnight the night of October 23, the music becomes louder and sweeter, and the very ghost of the man can be seen, fiddling away, with his little box of money at his feet.

‡

JOHNNY COYLE

Nice place, the Accomac Inn. Historic place, the Accomac Inn. *Haunted* place, the Accomac Inn.

The handsome, handwritten menu of the restaurant tells culinary tales of *Crêvettes au Poivre Verte Crème, Radis et Cresson aux Concombres, Assiette des Legumes* and a broad selection of other appetizers, entrees and desserts prepared with loving care by the executive chef, the chef de cuisine, and a competent staff.

The Queen Anne Dining room, the private dining room, the broad porch—each is set with distinction in an inn which has been recognized by *Gourmet, Fine Dining,* and *Bon Appetit* magazines.

Nestled in a nook carved into a hill which descends dramatically to the banks of the broad Susquehanna, the river view from the Accomac is breathtaking.

Nice place, the Accomac Inn.

Turning back the pages of history, the very first hint of the need for a hostelry on the site of the present Accomac Inn can be found in the early surveys, patents and deeds of Maryland.

On March 28, 1722, Philip Syng and Thomas Brown formed "The Partners' Adventure" and had 200 acres surveyed along the banks of the Susqehanna River.

Native American villages dotted the region, and the land was disputed by authorities of the Pennsylvania and Maryland colonies. Treaties with the natives, ill-defined borders and other considerations kept the claims of the "partners" in limbo for ten years.

In 1732, authorities in Maryland granted the patent

67

to Syng and Thomas, but the intrigue was not yet ended.

It wasn't until 1738 that the Royal Court in London stepped in and ruled that the two territories settle their problems amicably and define a final border line.

The colonies obeyed the order, and the "partners'" 200 acres of what was Maryland land were incorporated into Pennsylvania.

Thus, the land upon which the Accomac Inn is now located was the first true land grant on the western shore of the Susquehanna River.

Development was swift as settlers found their way across the forests and fields of the broad river valley and into uncharted lands to the west.

In 1730, James Anderson established a ferry between what is now Marietta and what is now the Accomac Inn. Forty-one years later, Anderson sold 35 acres at the western terminus of his ferry to his son, and by 1775, "Anderson's Ferry Inn" appeared on maps for the first time.

It is known that Marquis de Lafayette used the ferry, and likely the facilities of the Ferry Inn. There is little doubt that many more colonial leaders stopped by, although it was the frontier at the time and any written evidence is sketchy, at best.

A bit of intrigue touched Accomac during the Civil War.

The grave of an unknown soldier is marked near the inn.

Some stories have it that he was in a Confederate scouting party sent from Gettysburg to seek a ford across the river if and when the Union army burned the covered bridge between Wrightsville and Columbia. He was either detected and shot by a northern patriot, or drowned when he was caught in a storm on the river.

A less romantic tale suggests he may simply have taken ill, died, and was buried by a nearby farmer.

Historic place, the Accomac Inn.

It was during the Civil War that John Coyle purchased the old Ferry Inn. He continued to operate the ferry and his wife, Mary, tended the inn.

It was during the Coyle family years there that the Accomac Inn became a *haunted* place.

John and Mary Coyle's son, Johnny, was nine years old when his parents took over the ferry and the inn.

Johnny never did well at school, his father continually chastised him for fouling the ferry ledgers, and he eventually found a fondness for the bottle.

What he did know was the Susquehanna. A contemporary document termed him "the best riverman of his time, knowing every pot-hole and shallow for a mile up and down from the ferry landings."

Such positive public notice as to Johnny Coyle's singular distinction was generated, ironically, as the result as the disgrace he brought to himself and his family on May 30, 1881.

It was about five o'clock in the morning that day when Johnny sealed his fate in a downward spiral of events that reads like a plot from a made-for-cable television movie.

Johnny took the first steps on his trail to tragedy when Emily Myers accepted a job in the Coyle farm, ferry and inn operations.

Described as fair of complexion, full-figured and possessive of alluring, gray eyes, Emily was orphaned at the age of five in Chambersburg. She was living with a family in Marietta when Johnny Coyle's father asked her to take the job. Mainly, her task was to look after and assist Mary Coyle, who was growing feeble and riddled with rheumatism.

It was said that Emily, or "Emma," as she was known, was quite the energetic kind and would undertake any jobs which were cast her way. With little or no formal education, Emma was not particularly intelligent, but possessed uncanny common sense and a

69

strong personal work ethic.

These attributes could not spare her from what was to result in her never enjoying her 19th birthday.

"Johnny was fascinated by her appearance and her manner," Mary Coyle said. "She tantalized him beyond endurance with her coquettish ways at times."

Johnny was taken by her demeanor, her beautiful raven hair, and those steel-gray eyes.

He would tease her, often asking her to marry him. Whether to humor him or dangle him at the end of her feminine fish line, Emma usually agreed to Johnny's proposals.

Whatever her motives, Johnny took her acceptance seriously.

Nonetheless, Emma kept her suitor at bay. Her affirmative responses were not borne of love and sincerity. Johnny wanted more.

Emma was in the barn milking cows when Johnny made his decision to elicit the answer he would come to demand.

He confronted the girl with the final proposal, and the final words she would ever hear.

"I then told her I would shoot her if she would not marry me," Coyle later said.

She turned him down and added that she would never marry any man.

"Upon her refusal," Johnny Coyle calmly admitted, "I shot her."

A bullet ripped through Emily Myers' heart. Death was instantaneous.

As Emma's blood saturated the straw and the cows recoiled nervously from the gunshot, Johnny Coyle turned the pistol to his own chest and fired again. In his haste, the shot went astray.

Grazed by the bullet he hoped would have killed him, Johnny ran from the barn. His parents were still asleep in the house, some 50 feet away.

70

Johnny ran to the house and awakened his father. Through tears, he told of his cold-blooded deed. The old ferryman told his son he had to admit his guilt and turn himself in.

The elder Coyle summoned the sheriff, and Johnny went to his bed, awaiting the arrival of the lawman. Later that day, he was taken to the York County jail and charged with murder in the first degree.

On October 19, 1881, Johnny Coyle was brought to trial. The crime, and what was to unfold in the county court house, was on the lips of everyone in the region.

Johnny was never considered to be among the brightest of individuals, and even his mother was to later admit that while he was basically gentle and considerate, he was rather dim-witted and at times had an explosive temper.

On the advice of his lawyer, Johnny pleaded "not guilty" because of a "weakened mind."

The trial was spectacular to the press and public, but generally uneventful and predictable to the lawyers, judge and jury.

The panel of four farmers, one cigar maker, one coach maker, a merchant, a justice of the peace and four "gentlemen" took little time to come to its verdict: Guilty.

The defense team swung into the action of appeals, and after lengthy and complicated legal maneuvering, the new trial was granted, as was a change of venue to Adams County.

On March 5, 1883, another judge and another jury heard the case. The same verdict was rendered, and Johnny Coyle was sentenced to be hanged by the neck until dead.

More than a year later, on April 22, 1884, Johnny met his destiny at the end of a rope on the Gettysburg gallows.

The townsfolk couldn't get enough of what had become a sensational case.

71

Only 340 tickets which would admit the general public into the gallows confines were available, and the sheriff had no problem doling them out to the morbidly curious.

Doctors imported from Philadelphia came to Johnny's cell the day before his scheduled execution and pronounced him insane. This, the defense lawyer hoped, would buy the condemned man some extra time.

An appeal was sent directly to the governor's office, but a reply was received with dispatch: "The governor would not interfere and Coyle must hang–sane or insane."

Clergymen joined Johnny's parents in efforts to console him in his last hours. Tearful prayers melted into uncontrollable sobbing, with Johnny ultimately dropping to his knees and begging for mercy from the sheriff, who he said was now his only, and last, friend.

The sheriff could do nothing but offer faint hopes that God would provide the mercy he requested.

On the Tuesday morning of the execution, Johnny awakened to a breakfast of Susquehanna River shad steak. He appeared calm and resigned that those were his final hours.

Thousands of people crowded around the jail yard. Only the previously privileged 340 could fit into the enclosure, but some of them sold their precious tickets for as much as five dollars.

Johnny Coyle was scheduled to take the nine steps and position himself on the trap door of the oaken scaffold at 11 o'clock.

The sheriff of Philadelphia County had forwarded a ready-made noose to his counterpart in Gettysburg. The anonymous executioner was positioned inside the jail office, ready to draw the rope which was extended to the gallows through an open window.

At about 10:30, John and Mary Coyle were allowed their final moments with their son. A muffled sobbing

72

was heard as they held their only son. "The hot tears of deep grief and distress rolled fast and thick down over their wrinkled cheeks," wrote a York Gazette reporter.

Hands tied behind his back, Johnny was led by the sheriff out of his cell and into the compound. He remarked, "please don't let so many people into the hanging."

It was too late. The business of execution was at hand.

Neither the jury, the sheriff, nor the assembled witnesses could hear Johnny's last words. The district attorney, who was closest to him, said Johnny forgave his enemies and thanked the sheriff for his friendship.

That "friend," his hands shaking almost uncontrollably, tied Johnny's legs together and wriggled the noose over his head.

Then, Johnny looked toward the morning sun as a black cap was fitted over his head.

Regaining his composure, the sheriff clearly and calmly read the death warrant and commanded the unseen executioner to carry out the sentence.

At 11:25, a dull thud echoed in the jail yard. The trap door opened and the soul of John Coyle, Jr. was committed to a higher judge.

"At 11:45, the heart ceased to beat," related a report of the execution.

Later that day, Johnny's corpse was claimed by his parents, who had an undertaker transport it back to their home.

The boy was buried under an apple tree not far from the barn where, three years earlier, an 18-year old girl lay dead at Johnny's crazed hands.

His tombstone, positioned to face the big river he so loved, was inscribed:

My Son
John D. Coyle

Born March 15, 1855
Died April 22, 1884
Aged 29 Years, 1 Month and 7 Days
Mother Dear, Weep Not
for I am Not Dead
but Sleeping Here.

There are folks who would agree that Johnny, although very much dead, may only be "sleeping" at what has become the Accomac Inn.

What's more, they'll tell you Johnny's ghost rises from time to time to shoot darts of discontentment into the mortals who work and live around the inn.

After the Coyles sold the property, it became known as Accomac. Historians trace the name it to "acaumauke," a Nanticoke Indian word for "across the water."

The inn of today bears little resemblance to its appearance in the 19th century. A 1935 fire all but destroyed the old inn, and it was soon rebuilt to its former proportions.

Its owners at the writing of this book have carefully restored it and furnished it with luxurious period pieces. The inn has the feel of the 19th century.

It may also have a ghost of the 19th century.

Several employees have reported unusual events and sights inside and outside the Accomac Inn. The reports have surfaced often, and for several years.

"A number of our employees, our cleaning woman in particular, believe they have seen him in windows," confirmed Accomac innkeeper and general manager Timothy J. Bowshot.

"Things have been moved from where they were put down," he continued, "and we have some people who think when they've been upstairs by themselves in the

74

dining rooms, setting up, that they felt something or saw something."

The president of Accomac Inn, Inc., H. Douglas Campbell, Jr., also acknowledged that there have been sightings and senses of the ghostly variety at the inn, and the spectral suspect may be Johnny Coyle.

An independent psychic, unaware of any of what you have just read, visited the Accomac Inn, unannounced, at the behest of the author of this book.

"Before I was even across the Route 30 bridge into York County," she said, "I could sense a long-standing feeling of sadness about the place.

"I was pleased with what I found in this world. The inn is very inviting, the people very accommodating and courteous.

"But, yes, there are spirits there–and I'm not talking about the kind from a wine cellar!"

Spirits? As in more than one?

"Yes, there are three ghosts on the property, in and near the inn itself," she continued.

Remember, the psychic (who desires to be unidentified) had no knowledge as to the murder of Emily Myers, the execution of Johnny Coyle, or anything else which had transpired more than a century ago.

"I saw the ghost of a young woman," she revealed. "She said nothing, showed no emotion, and seemed to be mired just to the rear of the inn.

"And, near there was the spirit of an Indian. He was a trapper, and somehow was responsible for bringing in food for more than one family in a small village. He died of natural causes in the woods and his body was never discovered. It simply decomposed to the point it became unrecognizable. His is still a strong spirit. I got a name–something like 'A-kee-a.'

"The third spirit was that of a young man," she continued, and the writer's ears perked up as she did.

"There is a sense of, uh, futility, about this one.

75

Something went very wrong with him, and his ghost jumps in and out of corporeality. It's hard to explain, but I think of all of the spirits there, his is the hardest to explain and the one most likely to cause some kind of poltergeistic activity.

"It's an energy thing, of course. His is a kind of spiral energy that could easily be detected to the unaware person as a shadow, a whispering sound, or a cold spot.

"I'm a little uneasy about his spirit, from my psychic standpoint, but the energy is totally harmless. All three are harmless, but very interesting."

When asked by the author what the name of the young man might have been, the response raised the hairs on the back of the neck.

"I'm not really sure, but I believe it was John. John Doyle or something like that. I know that's a stretch, but that's the message I got.

"I wish someone could tell me more," the psychic added.

I believe we just did.

☦

THE WHITE HERMIT AND THE GHOSTS OF BUBE'S BREWERY

Some places just *look* and *feel* like they should be haunted. There's just something about them that seems to invite tales of "ghoulies and ghosties and long-leggity beasties–and things that go bump in the night."

And, while we borrow a line from a scary Scottish proverb, we burrow beneath the fertile topsoil of Lancaster County for our next story–into the dark and dank confines of the catacombs beneath an elegant restaurant in Mt. Joy.

To set the stage for this ghostly visit, the setting must be described.

It is Bube's Brewery Restaurant (Bube as in *booby*), at 102 N. Market Street. As restaurants go, it is one of the finest anywhere, and its atmosphere is unique.

Actually, there are three restaurants. The Bottling Works is situated in what was the actual bottling plant of the old brewery. In season, diners may opt to sit in the Biergarten, which is highlighted by the huge boiler and smokestack which once generated the steam power to operate the brewery.

Alois's is the fine-dining area. Luxury surrounds patrons who begin their experience with an appetizer and aperitif in the parlor and then move to one of the several intimate dining rooms in what was the Central Hotel.

An architectural and historical gem just off the

main street of Mount Joy, the old Central Hotel still retains its original hotel license, the 77th ever issued in Pennsylvania.

The third restaurant is the Catacombs. A serf dressed in medieval garb leads diners to their tables which are set in limestone-lined vaults more than 40 feet below street level.

Medieval Feasts are held on a regular schedule in this setting, and every Halloween the Catacombs are turned into a faux-haunted cavern for midnight tours and parties.

In reality, the management of Bube's Brewery Restaurant need not fabricate tales simply for the season of spooks.

There are ghosts above and below ground at Bube's Brewery.

Alois Bube came to Mt. Joy from Bavaria and brought with him his brewing skills. In 1859, he built a brewery on the present site, and it became part of a mid-19th century movement which made Lancaster County the "Munich of the New World" for several decades.

At one time there were more than 70 breweries in the county, but until the recent phenomenon of "micro-brewing," the Bube operation was the sole survivor of the golden age of brewing in the Pennsylvania Dutch Country. Much of its original machinery and many old casks remain intact, and visitors may tour what is considered to be the best example of a 19th century brewery in the United States.

With the Victorian setting of the hotel and the Gothic darkness of the Catacombs, Bube's seems to be a smorgasbord of the supernatural.

A look into the checkered history of the place and those who peopled it will add even more tempting dishes to this banquet of the bizarre.

Alois Bube's brewery succeeded for several years, but after his death in 1908, his five daughters and one son either showed no interest or had no skills in keeping the business alive. The brewery finally closed in 1916.

One of Bube's daughters, Josephine, married a man named Henry Engle, who most researchers feel was the one responsible for sapping the Bube family resources and driving the business into the ground. Henry and Josephine had two children, both of whom appeared to be on steady courses for success until things went very wrong and both began to display strange behavior.

One of those daughters of Henry and Josephine was Pauline, who returned to spend the rest of her life in an upstairs room of the old hotel.

"Supposedly," said Bube's Brewery Restaurant owner Sam Allen, "people still see traces of both Pauline, who died in the 1960s, and Henry Engle in what was once the family dining room."

Mr. Allen is talking about one of the most disconcerting types of apparitions–when an entire scene or setting is envisioned somehow intermingled within an existing scene or setting.

"If you walk by the dining room in what is now the hotel, you might look and see the room set up differently than the way it is now," he added.

"You get this quick glance. When you look closer, it's gone. It's very hard to explain."

Most of the ghostly activity takes place in the so-called "Peacock Room" which once served as the Bube family dining room.

Located just to the right of the main entrance to the restaurant (and across the hall from a staircase upon which one of the Bube sisters was born), the room now accommodates about a dozen diners and is appointed with splendid wall hangings which include colorful treatments of mounted and framed peacock feathers.

"The ghosts have often been seen in that room," said Sam Allen. "It's where we believe most of the energy is centered. What's really strange, though, is the way the room seems to be re-arranged in the blink of an eye."

Not only has the ethereal tableau been witnessed by guests and employees at Bube's, some folks have actually seen the ghosts of two very interesting people.

"Some people have seen *them* in there–the crazy daughter and the father," Allen continued.

"There's no rattling in the night, or anything like that. But often, in that same room, folks have seen those two ghosts. Everyone's aware of the ghosts there. It's always the same thing, an older, heavyset man, and a younger woman."

Allen quipped that the town gossips used to spread the story that in the 1950s, the aging Pauline could often be seen in the buff, through the uncurtained window of her upstairs bedroom.

No nude ghosts have been spotted in the old hotel, but Allen did acknowledge that something does haunt one of the upstairs rooms.

"Up on the third floor, in room number nine of the hotel–well, everybody who goes in there says it's just creepy.

"I don't know what happened in there, but they say there's a ghost in the room. I've been told it's a male ghost, but I don't know much more."

But, there is much more in the vein of the strange which lies buried deeply in the vein of limestone beneath the brewery and hotel.

Sam Allen continued. "There's a legend that there's actually a cave or catacomb *under* our catacombs. I've been told that if we'd excavate below the existing catacombs, we'd find two more. There are stories about how they were used to hide slaves in the Underground Railroad, and lots of other stories. We do know that there is some sort of passage which leads out to and under the street."

At one time, there were many large passageways

and caverns under much of Mt. Joy. Most of them were damaged or filled in as modern utilities and development took over, and the Bube's catacombs are just about all that remain.

Somewhere down there, another spirit may dwell.

They call him the White Hermit.

They called him that since well before the days of the Revolutionary War, and his story is part of Mt. Joy's rich folklore.

The gent was a teacher in Scotland who lived with his natural father and an evil stepmother. According to a story he told before he went into hiding, he was so mistreated by his stepmother that one frigid night when his father was away he forcibly removed the woman and her infant child from the house and into the cold. The next morning, they were both found dead, cowering in front of the door, having begged for mercy.

He fled his home and his homeland, and sometime around 1750 he came to America, ventured inland to Lancaster, and sought a teaching position.

Despite traveling 5,000 miles and settling in what was then a tiny village, the man happened upon someone else from his home in Scotland.

Fearing he would be discovered and turned in for his crime, he abandoned his hopes for a new life and took to the forests where he would live the rest of his life in solitude.

At what is now Mt. Joy, he happened upon a cave and made it his home.

He lived there alone, finding sustenance by trapping, hunting, fishing and harvesting roots and herbs which grew nearby.

For six years, the hermit existed undiscovered by the Indians nearby, or the white settlers who were rapidly encroaching.

When the first whites made their way to the entrance of his cave, the recluse emerged with long, unkempt hair and a bushy, matted, white beard.

News of the White Hermit spread fast. Most people kept their distance from the man and his cave.

The White Hermit became more notorious when something drove him to spend his waning years totally naked.

One story passed on through the generations is that the hermit saw a vision in his cave, and heard a voice which commanded: "Arise, oh man! Strip off your garments and go forth henceforth stark naked to and fro for seven years and atone for the damning deed done to thy stepmother and little sister!!"

In utter fear and compliance, the White Hermit then became the Naked Man.

While he still spent most of his days and nights in his cavern, the Naked Man was often spotted–in all seasons of the year–carrying out the command of the cavern clarion.

The last time anyone heard anything from (or, better yet, *saw*) the Naked Man was sometime around 1763.

Sam Allen has heard the stories.

"This guy was pretty scary when he was alive," he joked. He was really out of touch with reality, obviously."

And, Allen added that the White Hermit, or the Naked Man–take your choice–is another of the apparitional appetizers which may spice the metaphysical menu at Bube's.

"The hermit died somewhere down there. His bones are still in there, somewhere. He's said to haunt the caves under Mt. Joy, of which, of course, the catacombs are a part."

Do the prospects of all these ghosts frighten Sam Allen? Do they chase customers away?

"Oh, no, not at all," he affirmed. "They give the place character."

THE ROSE LADY
OF ALDEN HOUSE

The title of this chapter is reminiscent of the title of a romance novel. And, there *is* romance in this story–along with a little mystery and a bit of ghostly activity as well.

Gloria Adams came to Alden House in 1989. The townhouse at 62 E. Main Street in Lititz had been the well-tended office of a physician, and was as handsome as any of the other fine buildings along the main street of what is one of the prettiest towns in the Pennsylvania Dutch Country.

"When I first came here," Gloria said, "it was a very elegant home. But, it was a very *cold* home, too.

"In the process of putting my own personal touches in, adding and enhancing things, there was one particular room which had a heavy rose scent.

"When I would go in to clean, the rose scent would leave, but when I'd come back, the scent would be there again. This went on for three to six months, so I felt that whoever or whatever the scent was coming from was quite comfortable that the house was being taken care of, and was getting a warmth to it."

The aroma would fade in and out, returning in full strength, Gloria said, at times when she felt most stressed, angered or ill.

"It seemed to be concerned for me. There was never any apparition, but always some sort of a presence."

Gloria came to call this unseen force "The Rose

83

Lady." She would talk about her experiences freely, and some of the guests in the Alden House Bed and Breakfast operation told her they hoped they would encounter the elusive and aromatic entity.

That entity eventually became more evident.

"There were times when lights would go on unexpectedly, showers would run–particularly in one back room. Curtains would draw back for no reason," she continued.

In time, Gloria started to question the benevolence of the energy that seemed to fill certain spaces of the circa-1850 home.

She remembered the time a visitor from abroad came to the inn and had an experience with what could have been the true spirit of the Alden House.

"It was a very important person," Gloria stressed, "one whose name I could never reveal for security reasons.

"She told me she woke up to a presence which was laying on the floor. It was a very poor-looking boy. She could not see a face, but it was a troubled boy who was weeping.

"She thought she was sleeping, but told me that she shook her head, rolled her eyes and looked again. She was definitely not sleeping and the spirit was definitely there on the floor.

"Then, she said she turned away for a second, and it was gone."

What had begun as the innocuous scent of roses and the invention of the innocent "Rose Lady" legend had become a more worrisome power which, she felt, must be dealt with.

"Upstairs," Gloria noted, "there was always a very cold, almost sinister kind of feeling. It got to the point where it bothered me tremendously. I asked the reverend next door to please come over and pray for the house or do something.

"He came over, and started at the extreme top of the house, anointing and trying to cast away whatever mischievous spirits were there.

"We did this the whole way down the house, in every room, and the day after he did it, *all you-know-what* broke out!

"Something happened to just about every toilet, we could not get the showers to shut off all the way, the curtains fell down, and other things."

These pesky problems continued for about three days, Gloria said, and then everything came to a complete halt.

Are the spirits of the Rose Lady or the sad boy still in the Alden House? Gloria Adams says things have been pretty quiet since she combined her own, strong faith and will with the blessings bestowed by the minister.

Still, she keeps her ears perked for any unexplained sounds, her eyes open in case the weeping lad's ghost would come again, and her nose ready should the Rose Lady make another fragrant visit.

✠

MANHEIM SPOOKS

Nobody liked to hear a good ghost story more than John D. Kendig. And, nobody *told* a good ghost story any better than John D. Kendig.

Given some time and a little prompting, Kendig could regale the listener with tale after tale–some not as tall as others–about the legends and lore of his beloved Lancaster County.

Kendig, a well-known historian, writer, lecturer and teacher from Manheim, maintained a vast collection of stories, photographs, and clippings and his mind was a bottomless pit of oral traditions in every segment of life in the Pennsylvania Dutch Country.

His book, *Lancaster County Waysides*, is a collection of these stories, and is a local classic.

As he rummaged through stacks of ancient documents, notes and newspaper articles, Kendig was gracious enough to share any and all stories of the supernatural with Gary Lee Clothier, who researched much of the information in this book.

Although he admitted he doesn't particularly believe in ghosts, he relishes the idea that there could be cognizant life after death.

"I can't see why there couldn't be ghosts, especially in places where people lived, died, and places they loved so much," he said.

"It appeals to me."

Kendig recognized the many superstitions which are strong elements within Pennsylvania Dutch Country folklore, and was himself not immune to the apparent fascination and, perhaps, fear of "spooks" which is inherent in anyone who has lived more than 80 years in this storied land.

"I came home about ten o'clock one night," Kendig recalled, "and just for fun I started reading ghost stories. Well, about midnight, I went to take the garbage out. Now, I'm half asleep, I'd been reading ghost stories, it was dark, and everything was very quiet outside.

"Then, I see a white figure right above me. It was just as if a ghost materialized right up from the ground. I looked up cautiously and I thought, 'my God, it *is* a ghost!'

"Here, it was the next door lady on her upstairs porch, standing there in a white night gown and night cap. I laughed. She made the perfect ghost!"

Kendig often shared his many ghost stories with others at club meetings, in adult classes he taught, and sitting around the Manheim Historical Society in the old town train station.

Several of the stories–whether they were based on fact or fancy–were passed on by friends, neighbors and relatives.

His grandmother swore the story of what could be called the Pump Lady was true.

"We lived in a big house on the square," Kendig began. "My grandmother was sitting up there on the porch, early one evening, and right out from our place there was the town pump, right in the middle of the street."

The town square was once the center for much activity in Manheim. It was the crossroads of traffic, commerce and gossip, and in that small town, everyone generally knew one another.

"That night, as my grandmother sat there, though, she had a funny feeling. Well, she looked up once and saw there was an old woman she'd never seen before coming up to the pump.

87

"She watched as this stranger pumped. She wondered who she was–and as she did, POOF!, the lady at the pump just disappeared!"

When Manheim borough beautified its center square several years ago, it returned the town pump near where it existed when the Pump Lady was seen. Perhaps to those who choose to maintain a vigil, this phantom still can be seen there.

A story told by and to several generations of Manheim residents is that of a mysterious figure which once prowled the streets of town–an ominous gent they called The Cloak Man.

In the earlier part of the 20th century, the streets of Manheim were not bathed with the glow of streetlights as they are today.

When night fell, the town took on a surrealistic character. The silvery glow of the full moon cast eerie shadows, and even though Manheim was a small and friendly town, it was foreboding after the sun went down.

It was then when The Cloak Man would prowl the dark streets and alleys of town.

Nobody ever knew who the true identity of The Cloak Man, or if indeed there was a human form inside the black shroud.

He would often be seen skulking in the shadows on Bull Alley (Ferdinand Street), and many a Manheim woman would report being approached–at a fair but fearful distance–by the faceless figure.

John Kendig also mentioned an old restaurant at Charlotte and Ferdinand Street, near the Episcopal Church, at which patrons and employees often reported strange sounds and slowly turning door knobs.

The door knob mystery was solved–it happened that a cat had learned to paw the knob, and was strong enough to give it half a turn.

What could not be explained as easily were the

heavy footfalls heard on the stairs, or the many occasions when folks reported feeling a presence and even seeing shadowy figures within the walls of the old restaurant.

"They blamed it on spooks," said Kendig.

"Another old story is about the old Washington House Hotel at the corner of Market Square and Charlotte," Kendig remembered.

"There was a little off-set building attached to it which was sometimes used as a barber shop, sometimes a saloon.

"Some of the town fellows would go in there, and they'd like to gamble. They'd play cards for money. Somehow, word got out about this and townsfolk would tell them to stop, or they'd get in trouble.

"Of course, they ignored the warning. Then, one time they were in there. There was a pretty big pile of money on the card table.

"All of a sudden, they heard a racket. They looked toward the door, and it started to open, slowly. Then, in burst the Devil himself! Old Satan scared the, uh, heck out of them and they watched as he scooped up all the money and ran.

"It turned out that a local man got the butcher to fix him up with cloven hooves and horns and all, and he got all dressed up to scare the men," Kendig laughed.

Kendig remembered yet another story which was told in what was a poor section just south of Manheim known as Buchtown.

"In the dialect, he was 'Der Nockisher Mon," or "the naked man."

Not to be confused with the *au naturel* cave man in previous passages, this naked wraith was a ghost said to inhabit Buchtown just after the turn of the century.

The story came to John Kendig from William S. Rice, a Manheim native who studied under the renowned illustrator Howard Pyle and went on to a career which brought him international acclaim as a painter, print maker and writer.

Rice, who died at 90 in Oakland, California, also collected Lancaster County folklore and shared it with readers of his columns in local newspapers.

The story of the naked man of Buchtown came from one of Will Rice's neighbors, Mary Ann Litzenberger, of whom Rice said, "she was a staunch Christian and we felt she would not stoop to tell an untruth."

Rice paraphrased his neighbor's recounting of the tale.

"When I was in my teens my two sisters Adaline and Rebecka decided one July day to go blackberry hunting.

"We went down the Lancaster Pike about a half-mile below the toll gate, to Buchtown.

"We had been picking for about an hour when we decided to rest a bit. My sisters walked on a short way ahead of me and I stayed behind to clean up some of the bushes they had overlooked.

"To my astonishment as I gazed across the field nearby, I saw the ghost of a stark-naked man rise up from a fence corner and slowly walk across the field, not looking right nor left, but having a worried look on his face.

"I yelled with all my might to my sisters, saying in Dutch, 'A nockisher mon! Don't you see him?' But they insisted they didn't see anything of the kind."

Mrs. Litzenberger then ran down the road to a farmhouse and related her experience to the woman of the house.

"She informed me there really was such a spook, that she had seen it too, at different times. She explained that there had been a dispute about the correct line of the property, and the ghost of the farmer-owner verified it by stepping it off where it should be."

In the southern end of Manheim, the shouts and calls of Indians could be heard in and around

Kauffman's Park, and many stories sprang from the old Hostetter Brick Yard which stood on the south side of East High Street.

Evil spirits and witches were said to congregate in the brickyard, and the ghost of a young man who hanged himself from the limb of a tree there was often seen by workers.

Rice's grandmother was a fount of phantasmal knowledge.

She spoke of a barber shop on South Prussian Street, which for many years was haunted by its former tenant, Billie Sheffler.

So haunted was the old room that nobody could or would live in it for any length of time. Finally, a barber from out of town found it acceptable for his purposes. Even when told of the alleged haunting, he scoffed.

For several months, there were no incidents and the new barber was building a solid clientele. Then, one winter night, a sudden noise rattled his sleep. In an instant, he heard a man's voice coming, as if from nowhere.

"Will you be shaved?," it called. It repeated: "Will you be shaved?"

On reflex, he shouted, "Who are you?" There was no response.

Despite some attempts to rationalize the incident and its possible causes, nothing could ever fully explain this singular incident.

Between Will Rice and John Kendig, there are volumes of stories which, for space limitations, must be left untold.

We leave Manheim via Lebanon County in which one of Kendig's favorite stories is said to have taken place.

It was a little house far from civilization, on the edge of a large swamp. It had gained notoriety as being haunted, and its latest tenant, another brave soul who eschewed the supernatural, had lived there ever so briefly before the resident wraith introduced itself.

John Kendig filled in the details.

"He was there a couple days, and all was well. But about the third or fourth night he slept there by himself, he had a funny feeling there was something going on around him, but he couldn't see anything except the shadows of tree limbs and only heard strange, funny noises.

"Then, one night he thought he felt the presence of somebody in the room. It kept on getting worse and the next night, he felt somebody touch him.

"He looked up. It was a ghost!

"The ghost tried to get a hold of his arm and pull him out of bed. He tussled with it and it disappeared.

"This went on a couple nights and he figured he'd have to do one of two things—he's have to go with the ghost and see what it wanted, or get out of the house. Well, he decided to go with the ghost.

"The next night, the spirit came again. The man followed the ghost upstairs into the attic. In a corner by the chimney there was some kind of little bar laying there.

"He took the bar and dug out one of the stones of the wall, and he found a bag of money.

"The minute he opened that bag and saw the money, the ghost flew out a window!

"The story was that there was a man who had lived there, and had gotten the money illegally. He hid it and horded it, and died without anyone else knowing where it was.

"That ghost, of course, was that man. As soon as it found someone to claim the money, it could rest in peace."

As mentioned earlier, John Kendig found much fascination in ghosts, but could not say he actually believed they exist.

Still, he remained philosophical and optimistic about whatever may await us after death.

"Well," he mused, "if I could come back, it would be as a tree. Then, I could just sit there and look out over this beautiful Lancaster County countryside, just as I did every day in life."

‡

THE SHRINE

Sometimes, a little thought, a little reflection can bring a hazy and horrifying situation into clearer focus.

That, indeed, is the focus of this story.

Jenny told her story as her children and her sister, Gerri, sat with her in the living room of her spacious, three-story row home in Lebanon.

That home has been in the family for several generations. It is a fact which should be remembered as Jenny's story plays out.

"I've always felt like there was some presence in the house," Jenny began. "But, it's never really frightened me as it has lately."

Jenny couldn't place the first time she experienced any untoward activity in the house. "I just blew it off as my imagination at first," she said.

"But recently, I've been seeing shadows going up and down the stairs–and mainly when I'm alone late at night, when everybody else is asleep."

She recalled that it was a period of about three months prior to our interview that unexplainable incidents seemed to increase in intensity and frequency.

"I'd go down in the basement and I'd feel that somebody was watching me. It's to the point now that it frightens me; that if I don't get out of that basement, something's going to happen to me.

"Even while I'm down there and I feel the presence, the cat goes crazy–it runs back and forth and back and forth and jumps up onto the rafters."

94

Jenny has even resorted to fleeing upstairs when the sensation that someone is peering over her shoulder becomes overbearing.

She has abandoned her laundry work in the basement, run up the stairs and shoved a chair against the basement door to keep whatever was down there, down there.

"As if that's going to stop anything," she nervously chuckled.

Her husband knows of her experiences, and was once present in the living room when Jenny traced the path of a dark shadow she saw ascend the staircase from the living room to the second floor bedroom area. He saw nothing.

Jenny was, at worst, uncomfortable and confused by what she had felt in the basement. Just prior to her talk with the authors of this book, however, any apprehension she had turned to fear.

"The other night I was upstairs, ready to give the girls their baths," she said. "I was standing almost in the doorway of my front bedroom.

"My kids were arguing about something, and I turned my head toward them.

"I felt something hit my head, and I was ready to turn around and yell at my three year-old. I realized quickly, of course, that she can't reach my head. Even if she jumped up, she couldn't reach my head if she tried.

"Then, I got scared. I grabbed her arm, we ran out the door and I closed the bedroom door behind me.

"Well, I opened the door again because I thought maybe I had left a lit cigarette in the bedroom. I checked. I hadn't."

Jenny then thought something might have fallen from the ceiling and struck her head. She looked up, down, all around, and found nothing.

She began to calm down, and gathered the children to resume their baths.

95

Just as she was preparing her daughters for their baths, she remembered that their hairbrush was in her bedroom.

"Out in the hall, I went to turn the knob of the bedroom door. As I was holding the knob, I felt someone lock it from inside. That door can only be locked if a button *inside* is pressed in. I know I didn't lock it before, and I couldn't have then."

Jenny kept a grip on the door knob and called for her mother. Sensing her daughter's fear, her mother summoned aid and comfort from a neighbor.

When that neighbor arrived, the three women searched the house. Nothing was awry. They managed to unlock the bedroom door and found nothing disturbed.

Jenny's husband returned home about an hour later, and had another look around. He found nothing.

Jenny was at a loss to explain any of the events which had tormented her in the past three months. The conversation turned from those experiences to more pleasant times in the big house.

Jenny and Gerri recalled their younger years in the house, and their eccentric grandmother's unusual habits and lifestyle.

Their grandmother's bedroom was packed with the icons, statuettes and symbols of her devout Catholicism.

Madonnas, pictures and carvings of Christ and saints, a replica of Michelangelo's Pieta—these and many more items adorned the chamber.

"We called it 'the shrine,'" Jenny and Gerri said, with fond remembrances of their grandmother's quirks.

"She would pray up there, in that room, for hours," Gerri said. "She would talk to God and deceased relatives, and it was a regular ritual."

She also insisted that the bedroom door be locked whenever she wasn't in there, so nobody would disturb her possessions.

The women noted a particular red velvet couch their grandmother took particular pride in. "We couldn't sit on that couch if we were wearing jeans, because she felt the studs might damage it. She kept it covered in clear plastic to protect it. She loved and was fanatical about that couch!"

As the women talked, they remembered some facts which may well be very important in relation to more current events in the house.

They remembered that their dearly departed grandmother departed in her bedroom–the same room in which the door locked itself.

They remembered that while most of the religious artifacts went into storage in the house–some in the basement– after their grandmother's death, it wasn't until about three months prior to the interview with the authors that they finally disposed of the old red couch.

The two women looked nervously at one another when they realized that it was just after that couch was hauled from the house when Jenny had her most profound and frightening incidents–centered in or near what was the grandmother's bedroom.

They also remembered how their grandmother used to playfully pat them on the head whenever they teased her, in much the same fashion the brush against Jenny's head outside the bedroom door had taken place.

What's more, they recalled one other salient fact.

"You know," Jenny turned to Gerri and said, "she always did say she'd be back to haunt us if we ever got rid of her stuff!" My God, maybe she meant it!"

Maybe she did mean it, Jenny, maybe she did.

"That might explain a lot," Jenny concluded.

Maybe it would, Jenny...maybe it would!

✠

THE WALKING TOMBSTONE

All right, it's not really a walking *tombstone*, per se. But what it is could be even more frightening.

It's one of Lancaster's most famous ghost stories, and since it is set in one of Lancaster's most famous cemeteries, it is even more frightening.

It is, more precisely, the "Walking Statue" of Lancaster Cemetery.

Tombstones, memorials and monuments of all dimensions and design are laid out in circular patterns throughout the 22-acre cemetery which is bordered by, among other streets, Lemon and Lime.

Situated in the northeastern corner of Lancaster city, the cemetery was first designed upon ten acres of the David Longenecker farm in 1847. Its first burial was the following year.

Near the entrance is what was the first tombstone:

June 6, 1848

Alice Louisa

Daughter of

David and Margaret King

1 Year, 1 Month, 10 Days Old

Civil War heroes, artists, industrial and agricultural pioneers, and folks of all strata of life are in eternal rest in the Lancaster Cemetery.

98

One of the most famous monuments in the cemetery towers over the grave of a young woman whose death and burial have become engraved in the annals of the mysteries—and, yes, the ghosts—of Lancaster.

If fairly-well documented indications about the sculptor of the life-sized statue are true, the work is worthy of any fine arts gallery.

Depicted is a beautiful, young woman dressed in a flowing robe or gown. In her left hand is a bouquet of flowers, probably lilies.

She is descending steps, and on the uppermost level is a half-finished column which is girdled by sculpted vines and inscribed:

Augusta Harriet
Daughter of Charles W. and Amelia Bitner
1884-1906
Could Love Have Kept Her?

Regarded as wealthy and in deep remorse after the loss of their child, the Bitners reportedly paid $27,000 to the Philadelphia sculptor Augustus St. Gaudens to design a suitable memorial.

The result is a provocative depiction of a serene maiden, her face cast toward the ground, next to a column—perhaps a metaphor for a life—only half completed.

If the speculation regarding the sculptor isn't enough, the cryptic and sad last line of the epitaph leaves much to the imagination.

But, the most intriguing mystery about young Augusta Bitner and the statue which stands over her remains is how the monument came to be known as "The Walking Statue."

There are indications that Augusta was married to a man named Tevis, but there is *no* indication on her grave that he ever existed. He is not buried in Lancaster Cemetery.

While there have been those who have refuted it, a long-standing story about Augusta is that she actually died *on the way* to her wedding or even *on* her wedding night.

It is said Augusta fell in love with a man her parents rejected and preferred she not marry.

Despite their objections, she went ahead with the wedding plans.

Some say it was on the eve of her wedding, others claim it was the night of her wedding—but either way, it was rumored that she somehow tripped down the stairs of her home and died of a broken neck.

Descendants of Augusta have attempted to set the record straight, claiming they had knowledge that the woman died of either tuberculosis, typhoid, or another disease—not from a fall.

Whatever, the "...Could Love Have Kept Her?" inscription leaves much for debate.

Debate also centers around the bizarre legend that, on either the anniversary of her death, the anniversary of her wedding (which, of course, could be the same day)—or on Halloween night or under any full moon, the statue takes the final steps onto the soil of the cemetery and takes an aimless stroll.

That, of course, accounts for the "Walking Statue" moniker.

More likely, of course, is that it is the ghost of Augusta Bitner which perambulates the graveyard, and according to a Lancaster woman who says she has actually witnessed the phenomenon, the nocturnal stroll occurs on no particular date, on no anniversary, and in no predictable pattern.

Now deep into her sixties, the woman who wishes to remain anonymous claims she has seen Augusta's spirit gliding between (and through) the tombstones of

Lancaster Cemetery on several occasions, for many years.

"I don't care what anybody says," the woman swore, "I have seen her.

"Believe it or not, she is very much like the statue. She has long, wavy hair and is dressed in some sort of long gown.

"The ghost, or whatever it is, is difficult to see. I can't say I actually saw a 3-D, clear vision of a woman at any time. What I saw was a whitish, vague, but identifiable figure. It was a young woman, there's no doubt. I couldn't see any facial figures, hands, or anything that detailed.

"I go into the cemetery often, to stop by graves of relatives and old friends, and just to be in a quiet and very nice place. They tell me it isn't safe, but I've been going there many years, and feel very secure there.

"The first time I saw this, this *thing*, was many years back. I can't pinpoint the year. All I know is that it was just about dusk, and I was heading out. I thought I heard a whooshing sound off to my left, so I glanced over there. And there, and I know you won't believe this, but there was this milky, white form. It kind of glided or coasted over the ground. It didn't known any boundaries or obstacles. It drifted right through any tombstones or monuments in its way.

"Of course, I was a little scared. There I was, in a graveyard, and I was watching something I could only describe as a ghost.

"Then it hit me—the form looked a lot like the statue of the woman they said died on her wedding night. I put two and two together and figured it was the ghost of that girl.

"I know this all sounds crazy, but I know what I saw. And, somehow I calmed down real fast the first time I saw it, so I never got really panicky.

"Even though I saw what I saw, I went back into the cemetery many more times. I still do today."

We asked the woman how long the ghostly image remained within her eyesight that first time.

"Oh, maybe a minute, maybe three or five," she replied. "Time seemed to stand still as I watched. After it coasted about 30 or 40 feet away from me, never coming any closer that that, it seemed to fade away altogether."

Has she ever seen the image again, since that first encounter?

"Oh, yes," she answered. "I remember one time it was early in September and I was walking around to get some peace and quiet just after my kids had gone to school. I saw the same figure, and in just about the same place.

"Then, I figured out that if you'd trace the direction the figure was walking to where it started, it would just about be at the location of that statue of the girl. Whether that had anything to do with it, I don't know."

Does she believe in ghosts? Does she believe the form she saw walking through the cemetery could have been the ghost of Augusta Bitner?

"Well," she said, "up to that point, I never gave ghosts much thought at all. But I know what I saw, and if it was a ghost, so be it.

"If it is the ghost of that girl you mentioned (Augusta Bitner), so be it, too. If it is, I feel sorry for her. I've heard that some souls can't rest until they've made amends for something they did in life, or for something they left undone or whatever.

"If that poor girl's soul is doomed to walk around like that, and if she's not 'resting in peace,' I feel sorry for her. It's a tragedy. It's a shame."

‡

HAUNTED HILLS AND VALLEYS

One of the largest cities in the Pennsylvania Dutch Country is Reading.

Although it is probably best known to the millions of tourists who converge on it every years as the "Outlet Capital of the World," Reading is also the seat of what some researchers say is one of the most haunted counties in the United States.

Berks County is in many ways the sleeping giant of the Pennsylvania Dutch Country. While Lancaster County markets itself as the center of the "Dutch Country," based mostly on the predominance of Amish and Old Order Mennonite farms, buggies and people, Berks County is every bit–and some would say more–charming in its "Dutch" traditions.

Many of its barns are graced with "hex signs," and some of its oldest buildings retain such architectural curiosities as Witches Windows, Devils Doors and Soul Holes.

Tradition has it that fake windows and doors were painted on the sides of barns in an attempt to lure unsuspecting witches and devils to them. Instead of soaring through a real aperture and into animals, hay or straw which could then be "hexed," the demons would aim for the bogus bullseyes, crash into the barnwood wall and be rendered impotent.

Soul Holes were often built into the stone walls of rural farmhouses, just under the peak of the roof.

Normally they were plastered or plugged shut. But, when a death would occur inside the house, the hole would be unplugged to allow the spirit of the deceased to escape the confines of the building.

In Berks County there are two Spook Lanes, a Witchcraft Road, a Witches Hill, and a very strong sense of the supernatural.

The ghostly ledger in Berks County includes several restaurants, bed and breakfasts, historic sites, theaters and even schools which are haunted to one degree or another.

The legends and facts of Berks and Lancaster counties often commingle, especially along the South Mountain and the low, wooded hills which separate the Schuylkill and Conestoga valleys.

Much of the history of Manheim, Lancaster County, centers on its founder, Henry William Stiegel.

Stiegel was an ironmaster, and more notably, a glassmaker whose work became world famous.

It is interesting to note that there is no record whatsoever as to where Stiegel is buried.

Some say his body rests within an unmarked grave on the land of a relative in Cumberland County, some say he is interred in his native Germany, and others believe he is buried in or near his old mansion, Charming Forge.

Situated on a handsome position along the Tulpehocken Creek near Womelsdorf, Berks County, Charming Forge is the centerpiece of what remains of an ancient iron-making village.

Stiegel called the place home as his financial world was collapsing due to the failure of his glass works.

Secret rooms, dark and mysterious hallways, old slave quarters and a room where Hessian prisoners were held during the Revolution help give Charming Forge its historical character.

The undying (literally) love of its illustrious owner

helps provide the supernatural texture which seems to permeate the stones, wood and plaster of the old place.

Since the 1930s, stories about ghosts in Charming Forge have circulated in the narrow dell that fronts the broad front porch of the mansion.

That very glen has also been linked with its own ghost tale.

Still today, folks claim to hear the sounds and see the sights which accompany the story of an unfortunate young man who met his death at the bottom of the hill which leads to the old mansion.

The lad was a worker in the forge, in love with a maiden who performed domestic chores in the mansion.

When word spread of the discovery of gold in California, the boy decided to head there and dig his fortune from the rich veins of "them thar hills."

Sure enough, in only a year of hard work, diligent saving and determined loyalty to the girl back home, the boy put together a sum which would be the seed money from which their lives would intertwine.

He found his way back to Pennsylvania. From the depot nearest to Charming Forge, he hired a horse and sped to the side of his beloved.

Over the rugged hills he rushed, and his pace quickened to a gallop as he rounded the bend of the Tulpehocken and caught his first glimpse of the big mansion.

The horse seemed to sense his emotions and responded to every jab of his heel and slap of the reins.

The quick clip-clop of the horse's hooves echoed in the little valley as the boy urged his steed on.

Then, with no warning, the horse screamed...it reared up...the whites of its eyes glistened in the dusk.

Something had spooked the animal. It flailed on its hind legs, lost control of its balance and thundered into the dirt of the road.

Its rider, caught off guard and trying desperately to

right the horse, held tight.

There was no hope. As the beast staggered in the seconds of terror, the reins loosened and looped and wrapped around the neck of the young man.

When the horse crashed to the ground, the reins tightened and the leather sliced through the rider's skin, flesh, and spine.

In an instant, the handsome young man's head was severed.

His intended bride, at work in the mansion, had heard the ruckus just beyond the porch, and ventured out to see what was the matter.

She walked onto the porch and fixed her eyes toward the glen just in time to witness the decapitation of the man she loved.

Still today, those horse hooves can be discerned faintly as the episode plays out in ghostly form.

Some nearby residents say that on certain quiet nights, just before dark, the sound is heard. If the light is right, one may also witness the most harrowing of all sights—the dim figure of a headless horseman rushing through its eternal ride.

Other phantoms stalk Charming Forge.

Members of the family which owned and resided on the Charming Forge property from 1916 to 1993 claimed they have often had otherworldly experiences in the "big house" of the old forge.

Disembodied footsteps are often heard on the main staircase of the mansion. Doors open and close on their own volition, and shadowy figures have been reported in upstairs bedrooms.

Perhaps the most frightening of all was the experience of one of the former owners who swore that when she was standing in a long corridor which connects the oldest section of the house with a newer (still, 18th century) addition, she heard the muffled sound of a scream emanating from the area of the old summer kitchen.

Distracted by the peculiar sound, she looked toward the rustic kitchen, where she saw black smoke rapidly forming into a ball shape, some six feet over the floor.

In a flash, the ball of smoke rushed toward her, the muffled screaming sound accompanying it as it bolted up the hallway, just over her head and beyond her toward a screen door in a rear doorway.

She heard the distinct sound of that door opening and slamming shut, and she then heard nothing.

The odd occurrence took only seconds, but the sights and sounds of it remained with the woman the rest of her life.

Several months after the incident, research revealed that several years ago, a young woman died in the house, and the circumstances of her demise led the occupant of Charming Forge to believe she may well have witnessed the manifestation of the woman's ghost.

It turned out that the victim had been preparing food in the walk-in hearth of the old kitchen when she turned away and the fire caught her dress.

It was the days before inflammable material, and the cloth quickly burst into flames.

The girl saw the flames and tried in vain to beat them to submission. In panic fear, she screamed and ran down the long hallway–black smoke no doubt trailing behind her–until she reached the back door.

In what were to be her final moments alive, she swung the door open and tumbled to the ground. Rolling around in another attempt to douse the fire, she was instead consumed by the conflagration.

Her charred remains were found later, just outside the back door.

Some folks say her spirit is still locked within the walls of Charming Forge.

Speaking of locked, it is interesting to note that after the ball of smoke whizzed past the mansion owner, and the screen door out back screeched open and slammed shut, the woman went to check that back door.

She had a feeling.

Her feeling was right–that back screen door had been very firmly latched throughout the entire incident!

Berks County is known for the diversity and quality of its many restaurants, and several of them live up to their claims of "fine food and *spirits*."

The Inn at Maple Grove, near the Doe Mountain Ski Area and Alburtis, has capitalized on its ghostly connections for several years.

"Dine with the spirits," invites its sign and menu. On that menu is the tale of the inn's resident ghost, "Charlie."

Said to be the restless and unpredictable ghost of an Indian who was allegedly lynched in the broad fireplace of the main dining room, Charlie has been known to move utensils, glasses and dishes, and create enough poltergeistic energy to nudge and shove unwary patrons.

While cantankerous at times, Charlie is considered to be harmless, and has never inflicted any damage or pain on anything or anyone.

His antics can be quite distracting, however.

Not far away from the inn is the Longswamp Bed and Breakfast, another former ironmaster's mansion in which the ghost of a former tenant has been seen gliding down the spectacular central staircase of the inn.

In nearby Kutztown, the central building of Kutztown University, Old Main, is haunted by "Mary," the ghost of a coed who died in the building around the turn of the century and has been tormenting and teasing students, faculty members and maintenance staff with her unearthly antics ever since.

Other restaurants which have their resident ghosts include the Apple Inn, just north of Reading, the Old Village Inn in Morgantown and the former Brinton Lodge, near Douglassville.

The former is occupied by another ghostly Indian, whose faint image has been seen by several employees and patrons, mostly in a second floor room and window.

The old Brinton Lodge, more recently operating under a new name, is the eternal roosting place of several ghosts, including Caleb Brinton, who established the old "gentleman's club" there centuries ago.

His spirit has been known to tweak women on their derrieres as they ascend the main stairs.

Another ghost, that of a young woman, has been sensed in a second floor chamber.

The ghosts at the old lodge which overlooks the Schuylkill River have been investigated by several renowned psychics, and the haunting of the building has been confirmed many times by incidents which have been witnessed by owners, employees and patrons.

At the Old Village Inn, the ghosts of a carriage accident come to call every once in a while. Several patrons and employees have noticed their faint images in the main dining room, and at least one psychic has confirmed their existence.

No fewer than two dozen ghosts do their parts to give the Loom Room Bed and Breakfast, north of Reading, its special character.

Several of the spirits have been identified by independent psychics after the building's owners first noticed the supernatural events which took place there.

The ghosts of Berks County show up in all forms and in all kinds of settings.

The Oley Valley, a fertile and historic area just east of Reading, is one of the richest regions for ghost lore in Pennsylvania.

Around its covered bridges, meandering streams, country churches and quaint villages are farms, fields and forests which harbor many tales of the unknown.

The forlorn ghosts of young lovers are said to wander in and out of two ancient walled family graveyards near Lobachsville, and not far away is the old Keim homestead, where the ghosts of an angry old man and a portly young woman have been reported by many folks, from the residents of the historic site to a former township police chief!

And, the Yellow House Hotel, a charming country restaurant and B&B, is haunted by the usually tranquil ghost of "Adrian," a young woman who hanged herself from an attic rafter many years ago and has been "hanging" around ever since.

T he city of Reading has several noteworthy buildings where ghosts are said to wander.

The former Hampden Fire Station, now a condominium residence in the city's northeast section, is haunted by the spirit of a former fire chief who died on the way from the fire house to a fire call in the city.

Never making it to his "last call," the chief's spirit remains earthbound, and has been noticed by those who worked in the building when it was an active fire station, those who helped convert it to residences, and those who reside in it today.

Not far away is the Northeast Middle School, in which several unexplainable incidents have taken place. The building is believed to have been built over an old graveyard, and tradition has it that one or more ghosts walk silently and invisibly in its halls.

Another Reading school, Central Catholic High School, is haunted. The former mansion of the family which developed Luden's candies has within it the ghost of a young man who hanged himself on the front portico during its years as a family home.

C ertainly the most frightening of all the ghost stories and haunted houses of Berks County are those of the lofty, wooded heights of Hawk Mountain.

To be certain, more than one psychic of international repute has termed the supernatural energy on Hawk Mountain powerful enough to make it one of the most haunted areas in the entire United States.

This overpowering force that sweeps through the rocky outcroppings, thick forests and hiking trails of the mountain could well be traced at least as far back as the days the mountain was occupied by Lenni-Lenape Indians, who considered the lofty summit sacred. In recent years, archaeological evidence of Indian ritual and ceremonial grounds has been uncovered on Hawk Mountain.

This reverence for the 1,500-foot mountain, and Indian legends which enrich its earliest recorded history, may be the foundation upon which a solid structure of tales both tall and true have been built.

The mountain was given its present name because of the number of hawks (and eagles) which soar along its ridges during migration seasons. Once a fertile ground for bird hunters, binoculars replaced shotguns when thousands of acres on the mountain became a sanctuary for birds of prey in the early twentieth century.

The world-renowned sanctuary includes a fine nature museum, visitors center, several outstanding natural features and miles of trails and lookout points. The Appalachian Trail winds through part of the property.

The most enduring ghost stories which take place on and near Hawk Mountain relate to several events which have been linked by a swirl of energy that casts a spectral spell over the hillsides.

Those ghost stories are a book unto themselves, but several presences on the mountain deserve mention.

Just after the Civil War, a gent who lived in a small cottage near the top of the mountain admitted just before he died that he had waylaid and killed more than a dozen men who had brought their wagons up the mountain on their way to towns and markets in the valleys below.

The locals had suspected the man, Matthias Schambacher, of carrying out the evil deeds, but had no evidence to convict him.

Schambacher operated a makeshift "tavern" within the walls of his home, which still stands today.

As the story has been passed on through the generations, he would lure the teamsters into his lair with the promise of fresh mountain tea, wine or moonshine whiskey.

After the unsuspecting visitors imbibed, Schambacher took an axe to their backs and killed them. Most likely, he disposed of the bodies by simply dragging them into the woods and letting the creatures of the forest have their way with them.

More lurid stories have been passed on, however.

Schambacher had no pigs or cattle on his property, but some men who were wined and left untouched by his axe reported that the tavern keeper served a particularly fresh and tasty hunk of sausage with his liquid refreshments. Where he obtained the meat for the sausage can only be left to the imagination!

There are also stories, some confirmed by modern historians, that Schambacher had a particular affinity for the skulls of some of his victims.

During renovations on the old Schambacher property, shards of skulls were reportedly discovered in a barren well near the house. That old well is now the centerpiece of much of the ghostly activity on the mountain.

Schambacher confessed to the murders while on his death bed. In March, 1879, he died and was buried at the New Bethel Church at the foot of the mountain.

As the undertakers prepared to lower his coffin into its grave, what had been a pleasant day turned nasty and stormy. Black clouds rolled over the mountain, thunder rattled the valley and lighting shot out of the sky. One fierce bolt struck Schambacher's fresh grave!

To this day, folks who live in or pass by the area swear to see a ghostly, old man wandering in or near the graveyard. A faint blue-green glowing shaft has been noted wavering between the tombstones on several occasions by several very credible people.

The most powerful energy, though, can be felt around the old tavern. Seances, trance-mediums and psychics have revealed time after time that the house and the land around it is very, very haunted.

It is haunted by the ghost of Schambacher, some of his victims, and most mysteriously by the wraith of a waif who died under questionable circumstances in the house long before Schambacher moved in.

The young girl, believed to be a deaf-mute, still wanders through the house, and the sound of a pennywhistle she played in life can still be heard coming from the cellar of the old building.

Those who are willing to tell the stories of the hauntings of Hawk Mountain will also relate incidents which involve a dog and a rooster which were seemingly possessed by the potent energy on the mountain.

Even eerier are the stories of an elusive "great white ghost bird" which has defied the senses of even the most seasoned and reasonable birders who avail themselves of the natural beauty of Hawk Mountain, never suspecting the *super* natural bounty which lurks in another dimension, somewhere far beyond the limits of their binoculars.

The picturesque Berks County park at Gring's Mill, near the Berkshire Mall and Penn State Berks Campus is another haunted place in the Pennsylvania Dutch Country which affords easy accessibility for those in search of ghosts.

History documents an incident in August, 1869, in which a young mother killed her three children and then herself at Lock No. 49 along the old Union Canal near Gring's Mill.

Within days, and often without any knowledge of the crimes, those who brought packet boats down the canal reported unusual and unsettling sights and sounds at the lock.

A bicycling and walking trail now passes by the site of the lock, and even today people who use the park's many facilities have encountered the spirits of the hapless young victims and their mother.

Another dry bed of another old canal in Berks County is the setting for another ghostly occurrence.

Adaline Baver was described as a well-liked, charming and lovely young woman who lived on a farm near the central Berks village of Leesport.

On one of her rare jaunts from her homestead into town, she met a tragic fate at the hands of a brutal murderer who left her battered and mortally wounded near the canalside hotel at Mohrsville.

Adaline's killer was never brought to justice, but from the day her body was discovered along the Schuylkill Canal, reports persisted that her ghost could be heard and seen in the vicinity of the hotel and what was believed to be the site of the crime.

Indications were that Adaline was accosted near what is now a bridge over the Schuylkill River near Dauberville. She fled her attacker, and with every ounce of energy left in her dying body, dragged herself to the hotel to summon help.

Her body and her screams were too weak. Alone on the muddy bank of the canal, right around midnight, she died.

Several articles in the Reading newspapers following the mid-19th century incident presented testimonies of those who swore they had seen and heard the glowing form of a young woman near where Adaline was slain.

The most credible accounts were those of two horsemen who swore to have seen glowing forms and have heard plaintive voices echoing in the fields and woods near the crime scene—30 years after the murder.

"They killed me...they killed me...please help my

soul," cries the voice of a young woman from the tree line at the spot where the murder was committed.

Reports persist that Adaline's image can still be seen along the old canal right-of-way between the Dauberville Bridge and the Mohrsville Hotel.

‡

THE GREEN GHOST
OF BOWMANSVILLE

Somewhere in the hills that hold the valleys in Berks and Lancaster counties at bay wanders the restless and melodious green ghost of the Phantom Fiddler.

Stories told by seasoned citizens of the Welsh Mountains tell of an old mountain man named Isaac Kohlmann who led a mysterious life, died in the thick of a raging storm, and was somehow doomed to haunt the hills as the Phantom Fiddler.

In 1935, a Reading *Eagle* reporter investigated the recurring reports of the phantom, and elicited testimony from two disparate residents of the Bowmansville area who, in no-nonsense terms, affirmed that strange sights and sounds in the highlands just off the New Holland Road were nothing new.

"Folks around these parts fear the Phantom Fiddler," said Uriah Kohl, then a charcoal burner and self-described mountain man.

"City people laugh when they hear stories about the ghosts in these hills," the roughhewn Kohl continued, "but the Phantom Fiddler is no joke. He used to be a pow-wow doctor when my grandma was a girl.

"He still goes strong at midnight when the new moon shines on the spook house down in the clearing by the trail. Nothing will grow down there, either."

That "spook house," (a common moniker used to describe haunted houses in the Pennsylvania Dutch Country) was located at the far end of Kohl's property, and he lamented that he never could find a tenant for the place.

Kohl, who claimed to have been married twice and fathered 25 children, lived in relative seclusion. The "trail" he described led off the New Holland Road (now Route 625) just south of the Berks County border, several miles from any neighbors at that time.

While Kohl parceled out his information in the manner typical of his rugged individualism, a gent on the other side of the hill was more loquacious and filled in some gaps in the mystery of who the Phantom Fiddler may have been and why his ghost continues to be seen and heard in the woods off the New Holland Road.

"I have never seen, but often heard of the Phantom Fiddler down on the old Kohl farm," said country doctor Abraham Loudenslager of Churchtown.

"My grandmother, however, knew the witch doctor whose spook, they say, clings to his former homestead on the mountain. That was about the time of the Civil War."

Dr. Loudenslager said the spook is that of Isaac Kohlmann, a laborer and handyman who lived on the side of the hill just north of Bowmansville.

"When Isaac was still young," the elderly physician said, "he worked for a man in the valley. He was not yet known to be a witch doctor.

"They had a disagreement finally, I understand. Not a serious one, as the valley man thought, but serious enough to make Isaac throw up his job and refuse to come back to it.

"Shortly after this, hogs of the valley man sickened and dropped off one by one until six were dead. Meanwhile, one of his mules was mired in a swamp and broke its leg. It had to be shot. A cow died of milk fever after calving."

As the farmer's woes mounted, he sought help from a woman nearby who was said to be a powwower.

"The friendly old hag told the valley man that Isaac, the 'good-for-nothing hillbilly,' had bewitched his stock," related Dr. Loudenslager.

The powwower instructed the farmer to employ certain techniques to cast the evil spell away, and to paint a blue and yellow star on the side of the barn to ward off any other hexes.

After complying with the powwowers cures, the farmer spent the following winter with no untoward incidents disrupting his home or farm.

That spring, however, a frightening occurrence shook the man and forced him to sell his property and move to central Berks County.

"What really drove him out," recalled Dr. Loudenslager, "was the ghostly green light he saw every night in the hill man's (Isaac) attic! The valley man thought that there was magic being made there that would end in more trouble for him."

Isaac Kohlmann developed his powwowing skills and between "patients" could often be heard fiddling near his hillside hovel.

When asked about the circumstances which may explain why Kohlmann's ghost was relegated to the hills, Dr. Loudenslager could only relate stories told to him by others.

"They say his soul finds no rest because he murdered a girl who spurned his love. So, he is condemned to play dirges at her grave when the new moon rises over the mountain spur.

"That weird music has been heard together with the appearance of a luminous apparition–a human shape with glowing red eyes, about seven feet tall, between midnight and three o'clock in the morning, I am told."

Even now, those who venture in those parts near Bowmansville report the glowing form and the eerie sounds of fiddle music coming from where old Isaac's used to be.

PHANTOM OF THE FULTON

When the marquee lights are ablaze, crooking their fingers of beckoning illumination, a theater is an inviting place.

When patrons shuffle down aisles and into their seats, the house lights bathe their anticipation that the show is about to go on.

And, when those lights dim and the curtain opens, the stage lights cast their brilliance on those who will transport the audience into a land of make-believe.

But, when the lights are switched off, when the last of the audience has left, a theater becomes a dark, almost foreboding kind of place.

By its very nature, a theater is a vault within which every human emotion is both impersonated and elicited.

Tangles of cords and ropes, tall curtains and backdrops which fade into high darkness, cubicles and trap doors and passageways–the classic theater is itself a fantasy world with its own tales to tell and its own cast of characters who have come and gone.

In the following story, we learn that some of these characters may never really leave.

Architecturally and historically, the Fulton Opera House in downtown Lancaster can hold its own in comparison to any other playhouse in the country.

To be appreciated fully, the Fulton should be viewed from a distance.

Then, the intricate cornice which is typical of the

building's Italianate style will be evident, as will the Hugh Cannon statue of the theater's namesake, inventor Robert Fulton.

The design of the building was derived from a design by Philadelphia architect Samuel Sloan, who also drew the plans for the old Lancaster County Court House.

The "Grand Old Lady of Prince Street" was erected on a site which may have some bearing on the mysterious occurrences which have been reported in the Fulton over the years.

Since before the Revolution, the Lancaster town jail had stood on that ground.

In addition to the obvious dramas which took place in the old lock-up, one very notorious incident played out there and was etched forever into the history books of Lancaster city and county.

A small number of Conestoga Indians clung to their lifestyles just outside of town in 1763, and they refused to become involved with the brewing troubles which became known as the French and Indian War.

The Conestogas were peace-loving people, and when rumors of war reached Lancaster, the remaining members of the tribe sought refuge.

They found their sanctuary within the walls of the jail.

On a Sunday morning in December, when the sheriff and most guards were in church with their families, believing all was secure and quiet at the prison, a band of ruthless vigilantes barged into Lancaster in search of Indian blood.

Their nefarious quest ended after they stormed the gates of the prison and massacred the defenseless natives.

The murders of these men, women and children effectively ended any Indian presence in Lancaster County, and added to the notorious reputation the Scottish Presbyterian vigilantes–known as the Paxton (or

Paxtang, in some references) Boys–built as they carried on their misdeeds throughout Central Pennsylvania and beyond.

There are those who believe that this well-documented act could be the foundation of the supernatural events which take place in the Fulton Opera House of today.

However, several years ago a group of students from Franklin and Marshall College initiated an archaeological study of the land beneath the theater.

Digging in the dirt floor of one of the tunnels which lace beneath the theater, they discovered the bones of Indians which, they determined, dated hundreds of years before the massacre of the Conestogas.

This revelation led them to speculate that the soil may have been an ancient Indian burial ground long before 18th century settlers built their jail there.

According to those who both work and play in the Fulton, many of the unexplained happenings there seem to be centered on the site of the dig and the massacre.

Indeed, when Lancaster business leader Christopher Hager bought the old jail for $8,400 and commissioned a theater on the site in 1852, he ordered the rear foundation wall of the old prison to be left intact. Some more sentimental historians would like to believe he did so to honor the memory of the slain Indians.

Hager's idea was to build a stately hall in which concerts, lectures and other presentations could be offered to citizens of the growing and prospering town.

Completed as the largest civic hall of its type in Pennsylvania, "Fulton Hall" fulfilled its developer's dream with its handsome main auditorium. But, the realities of life in an agricultural town in many ways still on the frontier of civilized America created a "special" atmosphere in the four-story structure.

The top floor was consumed by a shooting gallery. The basement was a storage area for a multitude of goods, including fertilizer and tobacco.

Lancaster County appropriated the theater as a site for court proceedings while a new court house was being built, and the Fulton became the source of much social and civic activity in the mid and late 19th century.

During a glorious century as Lancaster's premier performing arts center the Fulton played host to the likes of Mark Twain, Gen. Tom Thumb, Buffalo Bill Cody, Wild Bill Hickok, John Phillip Sousa, W.C. Fields, Al Jolsen and many other legends of the stage.

Audiences in the Fulton also enjoyed the road companies of many Broadway shows.

Renovated several times to suit the needs of the community and ever-changing entertainment tastes and technologies, the Fulton reached its present appearance during a renovation in the 1960s, when a non-profit foundation was formed to save the structure.

After a rather ignominious era and threats of demolition, the Fulton Opera House was honored as a National Historic Landmark in 1969.

The theater came alive again as restoration and renovations re-captured the dignity and integrity of the old playhouse.

When the dust settled and the lights shone again on the Fulton stage, audiences flocked to their new showplace.

So, too, did the phantoms of the Fulton Opera House.

Barry Kornhauser is the theater's historian. His task is to assemble events and anecdotes from the past and record proceedings of the present so that those in the future may better know the heritage of the Fulton.

Some proceedings which take place will never be recorded in the official journal of the Fulton. Some folks would rather not discuss them.

Still, it is difficult to deny that based on the testimony of many people, the Fulton Opera House is haunted.

From its foundation to the lofty "Peanut Heaven" cheap seats in the highest part of the balcony, the Fulton is awash with tales of glowing figures, disembodied sounds, and more thrills and chills than any show or film could ever have provided.

Kornhauser recalled the experience of one theater employee who had a very profound experience in the basement.

"He was working down near the tunnel where the Indian massacre took place," Kornhauser said, "and he came running upstairs, white as a ghost, shivering and almost in hysterics. He said he was down there cleaning and something very clear and cold passed right by him."

Who or what that presence may be, Kornhauser does not know. Another theater employee, who declined to be identified, is convinced that there is a strong energy in the lower levels of the building.

"I'll never go down there," she said. "I'm not saying it's an evil force, but it makes me very uneasy. I was down there one time and felt as if someone was looking over my shoulder. One time I turned around, and in the corner of my eye I swear I saw a face–two eyes, nose, mouth–the whole nine yards. I knew there was nobody else there, though.

"Call me superstitious," she continued, "but I think that because that gang killed those innocent Indians down there a couple hundred years ago, the place is cursed, or hexed, or whatever."

In 1992, house manager Tom Treadway confirmed the episode in the basement, and admitted that he, too, has felt the presence of someone looking over his shoulder.

In Peanut Heaven (or the Peanut Gallery, as it is also known), there have been many close encounters of the scary kind.

"Up there in the Peanut Gallery," Kornhauser

recalled, "none of the technical people will work by themselves. They get eerie feelings. They hear footsteps. They hear and see doors open and close, so people tend to shy away from the place.

"One of our technical directors was scared to death up there, and he was a pretty level headed fellow.

"Another place is down below the stage, where the private dressing rooms are. A few summers ago, both an actress who was down in the dressing room area and one of our employees was out there in the front of the house and both experienced something at the same time, each unaware that the other was having the same thing happen to them."

Just who the ghost, or *ghosts*, of the Fulton may be is a matter of pure speculation.

One suspect is John Durang, a Lancaster native who is generally regarded as being America's first native-born actor.

Interestingly, it was a descendant of his, Edwin Forrest Durang, who oversaw the 1873 renovation of the Fulton from a meeting hall to an opera house.

Barry Kornhauser also has heard tales by some who link the ghostly activity in the dressing room with the actress Sarah Bernhardt, who performed in the Fulton in 1912.

"For several years," he said, "Sarah Bernhardt's dressing room was preserved as sort of a tourist attraction. Then, they needed the space, so they tore it apart to use it as a regular dressing room. The incident involving those two women took place right down in that area, so Sarah is one of the candidates."

There is another theory, borne of a psychic "interview" conducted near a small staircase at stage right.

In that area, several people have reported the ghostly image of a woman dressed all in white.

One individual who claimed to have psychic powers,

asked the wraith her name. The ghost replied, "Marie."

Kornhauser's research revealed that an actress named Marie Cahill was a regular performer in the Fulton around the turn of the twentieth century.

Cahill was regarded as being quite the perfectionist, and was best known for nearly always dressing in white. "It was one of her trademarks," said Kornhauser.

There are other spirits in other sections of the theater. Some may treat patrons to shows they'd never see on stage.

"Before the theater looks like it does now," Kornhauser continued, "there had been a center aisle, and there are stories about a white vapor crossing from the back of the house to the stage, down that aisle, and then dissipating in the orchestra pit.

"I know two actresses on stage, who were in the middle of a production, who had to stop everything. They just went blank, and then they resumed the show after they gathered their senses.

"They were new to the opera house, and months later, when they heard the story about the white vapor, they admitted that the breaks in their performances were caused because they had seen that vapor."

On occasion, the house piano has been heard playing, with no human fingers on its keys. Workers in the empty theater swear to have heard the applause of a non-existent audience, and a ghost dressed in 19th century garb crosses along the front row of the balcony, from one side to another, before disappearing.

And, a female ghost, described as "cold and frightening," has been seen on a scaffolding which towers some 70 feet above the stage, just above a pinrail upon which resides a more docile spirit.

The Fulton employee who preferred to remain nameless said there's a certain character to the old place that seems to invite tales of the supernatural.

"But I know," she said, "that these are more than

just stories. Two people I know quite well, and who I would trust implicitly, have told me their experiences, and I have to believe them. One of them saw that white mist they say comes down the center of the seats. It was just the way I've heard about it. They said it hovered just above the seats, sometimes looked as if it was going to take shape as a human being, but just before it would, it would just go 'poof' down around the front of the stage.

"I don't know what it's all about," she continued, "but I gotta believe there are ghosts in here."

Then why, she was asked, does she come to work at a place which is haunted?

"Oh," she replied, a smile building, "that makes it cool. Sure, the stories scare me, and sometimes I've been scared myself. But stories about ghosts, the unknown, the unthinkable–isn't that what theaters are supposed to present?

"Only thing, in this case, the theater isn't just the place the story takes place–it *is* the story, I guess!"

Be they the pathetic spirits of the murdered Indians, the ethereal energy of the fastidious Ms. Cahill, or the ghost of the legendary Sarah Bernhardt, the phantoms of the opera house in downtown Lancaster help enrich the history of one of America's great entertainment halls.

‡

LAUGHING ANNIE

Call her The Laughing Lady or Laughing Annie. Call her whatever you wish. But whatever, call her one of the most fascinating ghost stories of one of the most fascinating homes in one of the most fascinating towns of the Pennsylvania Dutch Country.

Strasburg is more widely known for its steam passenger railroad, and for being the site of the Railroad Museum of Pennsylvania.

All of that is interesting from a tourist promotion standpoint, but it is also interesting to note that no active railroad tracks actually extend through the borough.

What does course through the streets is the charm of a small town and the challenges of the twentieth century which pit video stores against bed and breakfast inns, quilt shops against pizza parlors and Amish buggies against 18-wheelers.

The sidewalks of Strasburg are lined with beautiful townhouses, stately mansions and quaint shops.

Main Street (Route 741) extends east from the center of town into the railroad attractions area. In season, it is generally bustling with traffic going to and from those sites.

Things quiet down a bit on the west side of town. It is there, at 130 West Main St., where the Gonder Mansion takes its position as one of *the* most lovely homes in a town of *many* lovely homes.

B.B. Gonder doesn't live there anymore. Neither do his children, his wife, nor his spinster sister, Annie.

Actually, Annie never lived there. But maybe she's there right now.

Confusing? Stick with us. It's a story worthy of a soap opera plot.

They're all gone now. Benjamin B. Gonder II (everyone called him "B.B."), Mrs. Gonder, and dear, old Annie are spending eternity in graves inside a Strasburg cemetery. The last of Ben and Mary's children passed on in 1968.

There are new folks in the old Gonder mansion. And, just maybe, Annie has exacted revenge from her brother, nearly a century after he spurned her.

Benjamin Gonder made his small fortune on the industry which is most closely associated with Strasburg today—the railroad.

A railroad contractor in the late 19th century, Gonder lived in a fine home at 136 West Main for many years. And for those years, his unmarried sister, Annie, was welcomed to share the home with the Gonders and their children.

In 1905, the huge Victorian mansion with its two white turrets was built for Gonder, and despite its size, there was no room for Annie.

Benjamin Gonder instructed his sister to remain next door and care for the old homestead. Neighbors said she was emotionally shattered, having hoped to move in with her brother and his family in the new place.

They say Annie never really recovered from the shunning.

B.B. enjoyed only ten years in his spacious dream house. On March 13, 1915, he died of a heart attack and his lifeless form was found by his wife in one of the parlors of the mansion.

For those ten years, it was generally known around Strasburg that Annie Gonder was living a despondent and lonely life.

In 1918, Annie met her fate under what were

described as "mysterious circumstances."

"Miss Gonder had been in a feeble condition for some months with a nervous ailment," observed her obituary writer in the Strasburg Weekly News.

Annie was 61 when she either intentionally or accidentally fell into the Pequea Creek.

She had fled the care of a nurse and had taken a streetcar to a station just outside of Strasburg. From that station, she walked through a corn field to the banks of the creek, placed her handbag and hat on the exposed roots of a fallen tree, and plunged somehow into the water.

A newspaper account said of her, "Miss Annie Gonder was the victim of melancholia."

If the eerie experiences of the present occupants of the 1901 Gonder home are any indication, Annie's dour despondency in life has turned into a jarring jocularity in the afterlife.

In a 1992 house tour sponsored by the Historic Preservation Trust of Lancaster County, Julie Lawson, whose family purchased the Gonder house in the late 1960s, told tour participants of her unsettling but strangely comforting experiences in the mansion.

The registered nurse who admits to having "a fanciful imagination," has linked several details of the Gonder family history with occurrences which have taken place in their old homestead.

Julie lived in the house while she in her early twenties and was attending St. Joseph's Hospital School of Nursing.

She spoke of a woman's laughter which had been heard sporadically over the course of at least two decades.

"I would come home from my shift at the hospital, after 11 at night, and I was never, ever afraid in the house," she said. She also admitted that she never heard the laughing sound.

But, at least two other members of her family confirmed that they had encountered the unmistakable sound.

Julie's brother said he heard what could be best described as the cackling of a crazed woman at the top of a back staircase once used by household staff.

It was a day in the early 1970s, around 11 p.m., and the teenager was alone in the house. The laughter frightened him to the point that he spent the rest of the night in his car, refusing to sleep in the big house.

Julie Lawson's father also told her about a similar experience he had in the mid 1980s. He heard the laughter echoing from a downstairs hallway. He was alone in his bedroom and figured the chuckling was that of his daughter arriving home. It was not.

It was Annie. Or, at least that's what Julie Lawson believed. "We think she finally got her wish (to live in the big house with her brother and his family) and now she gets to have the last laugh on her brother," she told a Lancaster Sunday News reporter.

"Isn't it strange, too," she mused, "that only *men* have heard the laughter?" Perhaps, she chuckled, it is Annie's way at getting back at not only her brother, but at all men.

Julie freely admits that many of the stories she attaches to the big house are borne of her deep love and appreciation of history and mysteries.

"For example, all the doors into and out of the house are on the right-hand side," she pointed out. "We all wondered why there were no doors on the left side. Well, the house Annie was forced to remain in was on the left side. Maybe B.B. didn't want to make it easy for her sister to come in. Maybe they put all the doors on the side away from her house so they could watch her come all around the house to get in.

"Another thing, when workers there removed wall paper from the dining room, they found a silhouette which had been drawn on the wall. There are words with it, and we believe we read, 'I Am Mr. Shiner.'

"Well, they all said it was a man's silhouette, but I said 'What man? That's the laughing lady!' Okay, it's probably a man, but I'd like to think it's Annie."

One of the most interesting features of the house are its twin turrets. Imbedded in the stucco are tiny, sparkling, reflective glass.

"When one of the roofers was shining the glass up there," she recalled, "he found two faces, facing each other. He said one was a happy face, the other was not so happy. Who knows what the meaning of that is, or was? Maybe the workers who put the glass mirrors just had senses of humor."

Julie pointed out that five people have died in the Gonder house, including her own mother and father. "To me, when you live a life in a home like that, and the home is so magnificent and has been here that long and has been built that well, it's got to absorb some of that life force

"If you have a house like this and it *doesn't* have some sort of mystery to it," she said, "it's sort of a shame."

⸸

THE FACE

What many Lancaster County people may think is one of their most morbid ghost story may not be a ghost story at all.

Few folks in the county, and especially in the southern tip where Lancaster tapers between the Octoraro Creek and the Susquehanna River, are not somewhat familiar with the ghostly tales of one particular house along Route 222, south of Wakefield.

It is an interesting legend, and many people say it's 100 percent factual.

Just north of the Maryland border is an old house on what has been known as Carter's Hill.

Curtains and shutters cover most of the windows, but one in the attic is devoid of any drapings. It is within that window that the stone, cold, blank stare of a young woman has been seen by passers-by for nearly a century.

It is "the head in the window," "the face on Carter's Hill," or whatever whomever has chosen to call it.

They say the house was the home of a newlywed couple just before war broke out between the north and the south.

The man of the house was called away to serve his Union, and the young bride was left behind.

Day after day, every time a carriage or horseback rider would approach, the woman would peer from the attic window in hopes that it would be her husband, returning from the war.

He would never return. Cut down in a Virginia

cornfield, he died and was buried far away from his Lancaster County home.

The woman met her death quietly in bed. Her earthly vigil had ended, but for an eternity she would continue to watch in vain from the attic window.

It is that heartbroken bride's ghostly face which can still be seen in the old house.

Or, is it the death mask of a jilted woman who left the house after her husband left her?

That version of the legend maintains that the woman discovered that her husband had been unfaithful.

Not comfortable inside the house they had called home, she turned the property over to a relative, but with certain strange stipulations in the agreement.

Upon her death, she ordered, a mask would be made of her face and be placed in the highest window of the house so her adulterous husband would always be reminded of her.

Indeed, there was a plaster cast of a woman's head positioned between sheer curtains in an attic window for many years.

And, at times, those who happened past the old house would also see the blank image of a woman's face join the plaster figurine.

The stories spread like wildfire. It was the head of a mummy. It was the head of a decapitated murder victim. It was the ghostly face of the young bride. It was the death mask of the spurned woman.

In reality, just what—and sometimes who—the face belonged to was explained in the 1930s.

According to one reliable source, the head was a plaster cast of an unknown model, and had belonged to Henry Carter, a student of phrenology who lived in the old house just before the turn of the twentieth century.

Carter's daughter, Kate, discovered the pallid bust among her father's belongings after his death. On a whim, she plucked the head from a pile of rubble and positioned it in an attic window.

Every once in a while, Kate would sit just in back of the window and watch the expressions of those who came past the house and noticed the ghostly head in the window.

When someone new bought the place from Kate, she asked the buyers to always keep the face in the window, if they had a mind to.

They did.

The head kept its designated place in the attic window, and in the annals of Lancaster County legends.

‡

GHOSTS OF
TOWN AND COUNTRY

Virtually every town, township, village and city in the Pennsylvania Dutch Country has its ghostly legend which won't go away–its tale of things that go bump, that glow, or walk in the night (or day).

Many of these are skeletons of stories. As they have been passed on, generation to generation, the bones of fact and fancy seem to connect, but no flesh has grown upon them to give them vitality.

The research team which produced the book you are reading has collected files of these frameworks of folklore.

Many of the ghost stories we came across are what we like to call *"they say"* stories.

They say (fill in the blank) is haunted.

Haunted by whom?

No one knows, but *they say* it's haunted.

Who *they* is remains the unanswered and probably unanswerable question.

And yet, this elusive *they* help spice our history and our lives.

If *they say* that big, old, empty mansion just beyond the iron gate, on top of the hill between those two dead oak trees is haunted, you are likely to walk a little faster past the scary place.

Because *they say* it is haunted.

Let us now thumb through the files of Pennsylvania Dutch Country ghosts, legends and lore, and hop-scotch across the towns and countryside in search of those bony stories which clatter through our imaginations and weave between the words of our history books.

The old Mission Church near Safe Harbor, Lancaster County, fell into ruins after the old dam across the Susquehanna River broke and a flood devastated the area.

Prior to that, an iron works prospered nearby, and its Catholic workers' families were served by the little stone chapel. When the fortunes of the iron works fell, so did the numbers in the congregation. By the late 19th century, the church was closed and sold to a salvager.

Over subsequent years, several people who approached the eerie ruins of the old church reported strange sounds and sights. Some even claimed to have seen an entire ghostly congregation worshiping inside the fallen walls.

White Chimneys is one of the most handsome homes in Lancaster County.

Situated on Route 30, some 15 miles east of Lancaster, the old mansion is the most substantial reminder of a tiny village which was called Slaymakertown.

The name was the Anglicized version of the name of the first settlers, the Schleiermacher family, which had purchased the tract from William Penn's heirs in 1710.

They, and other pioneering types, built taverns, churches, and farm houses in the Pequea Valley and traded with the indigenous Susquehannocks.

White Chimneys evolved into its present over centuries, and its owners have always maintained the manor house with an air of dignity.

And, through those centuries of structural changes, the mansion has also accrued its share of ghost stories.

In his wonderful book, *Captives' Mansion*, S.R.

Slaymaker II alludes to the tales of his ancestors' spirits which are said to remain bound inside the walls of White Chimneys.

One of those wraiths is Henry Slaymaker–squire, friend of President James Buchanan, political insider, and outspoken opponent of slavery.

Henry Slaymaker had closely followed what he feared would be the dismantling of the Union, telling anyone who would listen that the slavery issue would divide the states and lead to armed conflict.

Less than a year before South Carolina seceded from the Union, Henry died in White Chimneys on February 8, 1860.

More than a century after Henry's passing, his heir and author of the family history chronicled what could have been a visit by the dead squire.

"I'd had nothing to drink on the night of my confrontation with the shade or dreamed image of my great-great grandfather," penned S.R. Slaymaker II. "Nor had I ever walked in my sleep before this event or after it."

Slaymaker said he had been reading on that late night in February, 1958. "About midnight," he continued, "I cut the light and dozed off.

"I seemingly awoke in the front room, downstairs, seated on a Victorian settee. The room was dimly lit. I remember wondering about this, for the lights were off and it was pitch-dark outside.

"I arose from the settee with both hands in the pockets of my bathrobe (I'd gone to bed without it) and faced the tall mirror that Amos had built in the forward wall. Henry's image, rather than my own, contemplated me.

"Older by far than he appeared in his sister's painting–my only means of recognition–the image certainly was Henry's. The hair was thin and white. Cheeks were sunken. A frock coat was draped loosely

137

over what seemed bony shoulders and a spare frame.

"Slowly he raised his right arm. The head nodded slowly, side to side. The arm dropped. He smiled. The teeth were bad, widely separated by dark flecks that evidence decay.

"The mirror's image was confusing. The raised hand was startling. The smile scared me."

After standing riveted to the image, S.R. found the light switch and turned it on. The vision disappeared.

Slaymaker touched on other episodes in the mansion.

Just after the turn of the twentieth century, tenants in a back room were frightened out of the place by what they described as a "death rattle" from the front bedroom.

Dim lights seem to walk the floorboards of the mansion, and other unexplained noises and sightings have caused other residents, visitors and employees to claim that White Chimneys is, indeed, haunted.

With reference to the only Pennsylvania-born president James Buchanan, it would be a feather in this volume's cap to report that the corridors and chambers of Wheatland, his Lancaster residence, is haunted by his presence.

They are not.

Several employees, volunteers and docents at the historic site were queried, and to a man and woman, none could relate any ghostly yarns.

As has happened often in our previous efforts, however, once someone who *has* had a brush with the unexplained in Wheatland will surface after reading this. If that someone is *you*, please come forward. A "book two" of these Dutch Country ghost stories is already on the drawing boards.

Interestingly, while Buchanan's spirit apparently has not taken up residence in his Lancaster mansion, it has been noticed many miles to the west.

James D. Van Trump, who co-founded the Pittsburgh History & Landmarks Foundation in 1964, was a regular visitor to Bedford Springs Hotel, a Bedford County spa built above a magnesia mineral spring around 1800.

During Buchanan's 1857-1861 presidency, Bedford Springs Hotel was the Summer White House.

In one of his studies of architecture in Western Pennsylvania, Van Trump noted, "It seems to me that the long echoing verandahs and solemn Greek Revival halls of the hotel are haunted by the ghost of President Buchanan."

A literary allusion or a literal conclusion? No matter...those who have read those words and then walk those verandahs and halls at Bedford Springs will ever look over their shoulder because *they say*–in this case Van Trump being the *they*–that the old spa is haunted by none other than a dead president!

And, speaking of Slaymakers, a ghost by that name wanders through the legends of old Margaretta Furnace in York County.

Located just off Route 124, east of York city, the old furnace was once overseen by an ironmaster named Slaymaker, and his spirit has been reported to be active near a small cave on the old furnace property.

The ghost reportedly was seen emerging from the cave and coasting atop an old, stone wall.

In 1953, nearby resident Robert L. Gilbert revealed that four decades earlier he and others were standing on a bridge over Ore Washer Run when they heard and saw a two-horse buggy come down a long driveway and vanish as it passed by them.

Also in York County, some claim ghosts manifest themselves in the area where Nelson Rehmeyer was murdered in 1928.

Several books and a motion picture were based on the killing.

Rehmeyer was suspected of being a hex doctor, and 33-year old John Blymire was convinced Rehmeyer had put a curse on him.

Blymire recruited two others and burst into Rehmeyer's house to steal his copy of "The Long Lost Friend" and cut a lock of hair from the old man's head. That, Blymire believed, would break the spell.

Instead, Rehmeyer resisted, and a fight ensued. The police report given by John Curry, one of the accomplices, was graphic.

It was about 9 o'clock on Tuesday, November 27, 1928:

When we got to Rehmeyer's house Blymire told me to wear gloves so that I leave no finger prints. Blymire rapped on the door. Rehmeyer stuck his head out of the window on the second floor and said I'll be down.

Rehmeyer opened the door. Rehmeyer had a flash light in his hand and while Blymire and I walked into the house, Rehmeyer lit a coal oil lamp. Rehmeyer went out for wood, came back to the house with the wood, placed the wood in the stove and placed a flash light on the table.

Just then Rehmeyer had his back turned and Blymire caught Rehmeyer around one arm and the neck. Blymire threw Rehmeyer on the floor.

Rehmeyer got up and went after both of us. I then started to help Blymire by fighting. The fight lasted nearly an hour. Blymire broke a chair by striking Rehmeyer over his head and that did not knock down Rehmeyer. That seemed to make Rehmeyer stronger.

140

Then I hit Rehmeyer with a pretty heavy stick and kicked him in the stomach and that knocked Rehmeyer down.

Then, both Blymire and myself hit Rehmeyer with pieces of wood while he was on the floor. Then we tied Rehmeyer's hand round his neck.

I poured the coal oil from a lamp over Rehmeyer's body and Blymire set a match to the coal oil. Before we poured the coal oil and set fire to the body, we poured water over the body of Rehmeyer and everything around the room except the stove to destroy the finger prints.

We set a match and ran out of the house.

Legend has it that down around Rehmeyer's Hollow, the old man's fiery ghost can still be seen from time to time seeking to somehow avenge his brutal murder.

Just across the York County line, where Route 194 crosses the Conewago Creek west of Hanover, one should not be startled if an entire wagon full of ghosts crosses their path as they travel over the bridge.

It was well known many years ago that the bridge, then covered, was haunted.

A story in the *Hanover Record* related the story as told by an unnamed witness:

Upon entering the bridge, his horse snorted with terror and refused to move forward.

The interior of the bridge being very dark, he did not clearly see at first what occasioned the fright of the horse.

As his eyes became accustomed to the

darkness, he distinctly saw immediately in front of him a large sleigh or sled drawn by two powerful horses, the seats of which were ranged length-wise and on which were seated, facing each other, probably a dozen men of almost gigantic stature, apparently military men, officers of high rank from their appearance.

The driver sat on an elevated seat at the front of the sled, with whip in hand and lines loosely drawn, as the ghostly team passed out it was so close to his buggy that our informant says that his lady, by reaching her hand out, could have touched it.

As it emerged from the darkness of the bridge into the starlight, it quickly melted away and disappeared before their affrighted gaze.

○

Both the man and woman later described in some detail the horses—"sorrels, with white blazed faces...their footsteps through the bridge gave forth no sound or noise and the sleigh moved as silently over the flooring as if being drawn through the air"—and the men, "no phantasm or creation of the mind, but a veritable reality, a party of military men, evidently officers."

A contemporary historian to whom the encounter was related (the newspaper clipping is undated) theorized the ghostly party may be that of Hessian prisoners who were captured at the Battle of Trenton in 1778 and transported to Frederick, Md., via that road.

Perhaps, the researcher theorized, a wagon full of prisoners may have met a tragic fate at the ford which crossed the Conewago there at that time, and the entire event is played out in ghostly form.

Somewhere between McSherrystown and Hanover, near the old wagon works, the ghost of Rev.

Contler, the first pastor of the old St. Matthew's Lutheran Church in Hanover, has been spotted.

One woman claimed she was approached by the minister's spirit in her back yard. The pastor extended his ashen hand toward her, but she refused to do the same.

Instead, she cautiously offered the phantom her handkerchief.

As the ghost touched the cloth, there was a flash of light. The spirit vanished, and the handkerchief was burnt to a crisp.

Supernatural events in cemeteries throughout Lancaster County and the Pennsylvania Dutch Country have been detailed in previous chapters.

Before we visit more haunted graveyards, it is interesting to note that the notion of cremating human bodies actually had its American origins in the Red Rose City.

In 1884, the Lancaster Cremation and Funeral Reform Society met for the first time, and published information about cremation.

Some of the city's leaders, including Andrew Jackson Steinman and J.P. McCaskey, were among the promoters of the organization and the organizers of what became the first public crematory in the United States.

Dr. Miles Davis designed the furnaces of the Greenwood Cemetery Crematorium, and later turned his attention to the technology of trash and garbage incinerators.

In its first year of operation, the facility cremated 40 bodies at $25 each (coal included). Supposedly, the attendant would alert children who lived nearby whenever there was to be a cremation, and he allowed them to peek into the furnace through a peep-hole.

This historical fact duly noted, let us now venture into certain cemeteries where the dead are said to rise and take nocturnal strolls between the tombstones.

Such is the case at the Hans Graf family plot, off Old River Road between Bainbridge and Marietta.

Within its stone walls is sealed a curse, and perhaps even a werewolf!

The story goes that he who walks around the walls of the cemetery seven times under a full moon will perish before dawn.

Further, Hans Graf himself is said to haunt the plot, and has been known to rise and take the form of a teeth-baring, growling, menacing wolf.

Across Lancaster County, near Ephrata is the ancient graveyard of Bethany United Church of Christ.

Established along Bethany Road, nearly a half-century before the Revolutionary War, the church grave yard has been recently renovated.

Its 200-plus tombstones contain classic epitaphs and artistic features, and many are etched in German.

One belongs to Sarah Wilms, the daughter of Rev. John Christian Wilms, who was the minister at Bethany from 1790 to 1802.

Sarah was 29 when she died in 1799, on the very day she was to marry.

Buried in her wedding gown, her sad form has often been reported gliding through the old burial ground.

An 1863 Reading & Columbia Railroad timetable listed among its many whistle-stop stations, one curious place called Spook House.

Old railroaders' tales have it that the station, nothing more than a water tank stop, was haunted. More than one engineer and fireman reported hearing or seeing "schpuks" (spooks) near the big tank.

The Pennsylvania Dutch Country is filled with many attractions of historical, cultural, artistic and architectural interest.

Of these, several claim (some with reluctance and reservation) that ghosts may accompany tourists who visit.

Sketchy information reveals a ghostly presence which has been felt inside the Lancaster Heritage Center in downtown Lancaster. The name "George Ross" has been suggested as the identity of the spirit there.

Across town in Lancaster County Central Park, there is a better known ghost story inside the old Edward Hand mansion at Rock Ford Plantation.

A native of Ireland, Hand came to Philadelphia in 1767 as an Ensign in the Royal Irish Regiment. A surgeon's mate, Hand served in Fort Pitt, Pittsburgh, and was discharged from the Irish army in 1774.

He stayed in Pennsylvania and set up medical practice in Lancaster. His political sympathies turned, and he joined the Pennsylvania Rifleman, in which he attained the rank of Brigadier General.

As Adjutant General at the Battle of Yorktown, he rode triumphantly to Philadelphia after the American victory, and then returned to Lancaster to further serve as a member of the Continental Congress and the Pennsylvania Assembly.

He moved into the stately Rock Ford mansion in 1793, and died there nine years later.

Although it is a showplace of Lancaster County history and visited by thousands of tourists, residents and school children every year, Rock Ford holds many mysteries and miseries within its stone walls.

Gen. Hand's own son killed himself in Rock Ford, and after the house fell out of Hand family hands, its later owners were hard pressed to find tenants who would spend any length of time in the old place.

One by one, renters would leave. Few would cite any reasons for their hasty departures, but those who did said the place, in the vernacular, "gave them the creeps."

Several psychics and paranormal researchers have declared Rock Ford to be filled with a depressed, somewhat demented spirit.

That seems to support the thoughts of one volunteer guide at Rock Ford.

The individual, who wishes to remain anonymous, says there have been several occasions when they have had the feeling that someone was staring at them. And, they claimed to have seen ghostly shadows coast across the floor of the old mansion.

The General Sutter Inn, named after John Sutter, the man who sparked the California Gold Rush of 1849, stands proudly on the central square in Lititz.

Today, a lovely 12-room inn and fine restaurant, the General Sutter was founded by Moravians in 1764 and called Zum Anker (Sign of the Anchor).

The present building is the result of an 1848 renovation.

Despite his claim to fame, John Sutter died a broken man after a vain attempt to find a cure for his acute arthritis in the mineral springs of Lititz.

His old Lititz home stands across from the General Sutter Inn. His body is buried down the street in the Moravian Cemetery.

And his ghost? Some who work in the dining rooms of the General Sutter will reveal their brushes with the unexplainable. There are those among them who are certain the spirit of old John Sutter drops by now and then to re-arrange things, create a clatter or two, and perambulate through the lovely downstairs dining rooms.

They used to call it Lard Lane (die Schmalzgass, in the dialect of the Dutch).

Today, it is Vera Cruz Road, just off Route 897 west of Adamstown.

For generations, the story of a ghost which has been seen walking across farm fields has circulated around the area.

The spirit, which looks at no one and says

nothing, simply wanders aimlessly and blankly through the fields, and vanishes into thin air as those fortunate enough to see him look on in amazement.

Gathering the lore of Lancaster and surrounding counties would not be complete without mention of the many strange creatures which have been reported by area residents over the years.

Some of these reports have drawn the attention of investigators who add the Dutch County encounters to the dockets of worldwide unexplained phenomena.

The Society for the Investigation of the Unexplained (SITU) in 1973 reported in its journal that two brothers in the "Big Valley" section of Lancaster County were accosted by what they described as a beast "the size of a good heifer, gray in color with a white mane. It had tiger-like fangs and curved horns like a billy goat, ran upright on long legs and had long grizzly claws."

The brothers were in their farm field at the time, and when their team of horses was approached by the creature, both horses reared up and bolted. The men were thrown to the ground. Neither was injured.

The next day, another farmer told friends he had seen a "thing" of virtually the same description given by the brothers.

The beast dashed toward the farmer, and just as it was about to pounce on him, the man lunged at it with his scythe. The animal–or whatever–ripped the tool from the man's hand, crunched down on its handle, and gobbled it up as the man fled in terror.

One more meeting of man and beast was reported the very next night when a woman at a nearby farm claimed the creature visited her farm yard and hurled a dead geese at her as it ran into the darkness.

In 1985, the Pennsylvania Center for UFO Research, in its "Creature Research Journal," featured the sighting in North Annville Township, Lebanon

County, of what seemed to fit the general description of a "Bigfoot" type of monster.

"It had no neck and the head appeared to come to a point at the top," the report noted. "The witness watched as the strange creature walked with long strides along a fence line to a county road where it crossed and ultimately disappeared into a field beyond.

"The figure's arms were unusually long and swung in unison with its stride."

A week later–September 14, 1985, the creature may have made another call to the rural homestead. Family members reported loud shrieking noises echoing from a nearby woods. The frightening screeches, unlike any human or animal sounds the witnesses have ever heard, continued for about 20 minutes.

Richard E. McGee, a Bigfoot investigator, went to the scene and did report the discovery of a series of footprints which measured 18 inches long. They were separated such that the stride of whatever caused them was more than four feet from toe to heel!

While some may think these "sightings" are the products of overactive imaginations or individuals craving notoriety, a check back into history will reveal many incredible encounters many credible people have reported.

In roughly the same area of the two brothers' harrowing escape from danger in 1973, many other incidents of terror involving indescribable monsters have been noted over the years.

So many ghosts and wretched, deformed beasts have been seen there that those who live there have come to call it the "Haunted Crossroads" of Lancaster County.

Apparitions included a ghostly white dog, a headless man, and a massive bull with glaring, red eyes.

In the extreme eastern corner of Lancaster County, California Road extends north from Route 23 through lush farmland and then rugged, rocky foothills.

Just north of Route 23 is the old California School, and that old building has been the object of ghost hunters for many years.

Built just after the Civil War as a one-room schoolhouse, its doors were closed for educational purposes in 1964. It was then that the teaching ended and the taunting began.

Rumors flew around the valley thereabouts that the corpse of a murdered infant was buried in an unmarked grave on school property many years ago.

A legend grew around this, and it was eventually reported that on a full moon, the mournful crying of a suffering baby would be heard echoing in the empty school and the yard around it.

From the time of its closing until it was purchased at auction in 1981, the old school became the local "haunted house," and nearly fell victim of vandalism and neglect.

It has since been lovingly remodeled into a home, but the story persists that the ghost of the child can be heard when the moon is full on California Road.

Call this final tale the "Ghost of Paradise."

In an unpublished 1915 masters dissertation, Isaac Shirk Simons recounted the testimony of a man who lived in the village of Paradise, on Route 30 east of Lancaster:

"A friend of mine once lived in a house which was supposed to be haunted. Every night they heard something walking over the floor of the attic. Then there would be a sound like chains coming down the steps.

"Then, the attic door would open and if no one would come near, the chains could be heard passing down the stairs and then out. They could never keep the attic door closed no matter how tightly they nailed it.

"Every morning that door would be open and it could be plainly heard opening in the night."

A FINAL WORD

We were not the first, nor shall we be the last, to plunge our magnifying glass between the lines of the history books in the Pennsylvania Dutch Country.

Others have ventured down the dark roads and into the deepest corners of Lancaster and surrounding counties to, in the dialect, "make the light on" which illuminates the rich heritage of this magical land.

To those who have come before us—to those who have entered the attic of our existence and have dusted off ancient tales, we extend our gratitude.

To those who are seeking and will seek to shake off more dust and turn the lights a bit brighter, we ask only that they respect what some consider to be the "dark side."

What you have read—and we thank you for reading them—were stories by and about real people in real places. They were legends which enrich our lives as a society. They were stories borne not of fear, terror or the "occult," but of genuine human emotion.

There are many more stories.

A thick file folder of story leads, clippings, telephone numbers, etc., awaits our perusal. We would like to think of this volume as "Book One" in our recording of the legends, folklore, and most of all, the *ghost stories* of the Pennsylvania Dutch Country.

Even as this book was being completed, a strange tale gripped the Pennsylvania Dutch Country as it reeled from the coldest and snowiest winter in its history.

From truck stops to quilting bees and radio talk shows, rumors persisted that a middle-aged hitchhiker foretold of a major storm which would dump several feet of snow on the region within days.

The winter-weary driver would take his or her eyes off the road ahead just long enough to glance over at the passenger—just long enough to also notice that he had vanished into thin air!

The mysterious hitchhiker was said to appear on main roads in Lancaster, Lebanon, Berks andYork counties. Even those drivers not prone to picking up hitchhikers under any circumstances felt compelled to give the man a ride.

After the disappearance, the startled motorists often reported the episode to police.

As radio and newspaper reporters sought out the details, they discovered that there had been no reports of those kinds filed at local or state police stations. Despite intensive investigations, no one who actually knew the alleged motorists personally emerged to provide more information.

The "hitchhiker predicts a monster storm" story was slipped into the folklore file under "urban legend" and dismissed.

But what you have read in these preceding pages amount to much more than tales told by whispering down the alley.

Throughout the Dutch Country, we have passed many an ancient farmhouse, Victorian mansion or old mill and wondered "is it haunted?" Time and space prevented digging deeper for whatever lay beneath the obvious.

If you have had any experiences, we invite you to contact us for what will almost certainly be a Book Two.

‡‡‡‡

ACKNOWLEDGEMENTS

There is no way to provide an adequate and complete list of all who helped in large and small ways in the researching, writing and publishing of this book. The following is a list of those resources which have supplied leads, information, assistance and stories. I apologize to anyone or any organization inadvertently omitted.

BOOKS

Lancaster County 1841-1941, by Frederic Shriver Klein, The Lancaster County National Bank, 1941

A History of New Holland, by M.G. Weaver, The New Holland Clarion, 1928

Of a Place and a Time: Remembering Lancaster, by Richard D. Altick, Shoe String Press, 1991

The Story of Lancaster, Old and New, by William Riddle, New Era Printing Co., 1917

Conestoga Crossroads, by Jerome H. Wood Jr., Pennsylvania Historical and Museum Commission, 1979

An Authentic History of Lancaster County, by J.I. Mombert, D.D., J.E. Barr & Co., 1869

The Long Lost Friend, by John George Hohman, 1819

The Geography of Witchcraft, by Montague Summers, The Citadel Press, 1965

Going Dutch, by William N. Hoffman, Spring Garden Publications, 1989

Pennsylvania Iron Manufacture in the Eighteenth Century, by Arthur C. Bining, 1973

Lancaster County Waysides, by John D. Kendig, Stiegel Printing, 1979

Captives' Mansion, by S.R. Slaymaker II, Harper and Row, 1973

Life and Architecture in Pittsburgh, by James D. Van Trump, Pittsburgh History & Landmarks Foundation

NEWSPAPERS

Lancaster Intelligencer-Journal, Lititz Record-Express, Manheim Sentinel, The Philadelphia Inquirer, Reading Eagle, Lancaster New Era, Berks County Record, Mount Joy Star, Strasburg Weekly News, Hanover Record, York Dispatch, Tri-County Shoppers News, Lebanon Daily News

MAGAZINES, JOURNALS, ETC.

The Pennsylvania Dutchman, published by the Pennsylvania Dutch Folklore Center, Inc., Lancaster; *Pennsylvania* magazine, *Susquehanna* magazine, *National Geographic*, *Creature Research Journal*, published by the Pennsylvania Center for UFO Research, Pittsburgh; *Pursuit*, published by the Society for the Investigation of the Unexplained, Columbia, N.J.

INDIVIDUALS, ORGANIZATIONS

Lancaster County Parks Department, Lancaster County Public Library, Museum Council of Lancaster County, United States Department of the Interior, National Park Service; John Kendig, Alan E. Mays, Gail D. White, Elizabeth Johnson, Gerald and Margaret Lestz, Beth E. Trapani, Barb Mundis, Pat Desmond, Esther Lentz, Rhoda Blank.

AND SPECIAL THANKS TO:

Gary Lee S. Clothier, whose original research, interviews and investigations set the stage for the publication of this book; David J. Seibold, who assisted in the research and compilation of information; and Tess, Emily, Kevin and Muffy, whose patience and support were always needed, and were always there.

Charles J. Adams III

‡

ABOUT THE AUTHOR

Charles J. Adams III was born, raised, and continues to reside in the Pennsylvania Dutch Country. "I'll probably die here, be buried here, and come back to haunt the place," says Adams.

In Reading, Adams is the morning personality on radio station WEEU. He also is chief travel correspondent at the Reading Eagle. His "Travels With Charlie" appears every Sunday in the Eagle, and a feature on ghosts and the supernatural, "Berks the Bizarre," is printed every other Sunday.

A past president of the Board of Trustees of the Reading Public Library, Adams also serves on boards and committees in several other civic and social organizations. He is on the Editorial Board and Council of the Historical Society of Berks County.

•

CHARLES J. ADAMS III
BIBLIOGRAPHY
(All titles published by Exeter House Books)
Ghost Stories of Berks County (1982)
Ghost Stories of Berks County, Book 2 (1984)
Shipwrecks Near Barnegat Inlet (w/David J. Seibold, 1984)
Legends of Long Beach Island (w/Seibold, 1985)
Shipwrecks off Ocean City (w/Seibold, 1986)
Shipwrecks and Legends 'round Cape May (w/Seibold, 1987)
Ghost Stories of Berks County, Book 3 (w/Gary L. S. Clothier, 1988)
Cape May Ghost Stories (w/Seibold, 1988)
Shipwrecks, Sea Stories and Legends of the Delaware Coast
(w/Seibold, 1989)
Ghost Stories of the Delaware Coast (w/Seibold, 1990)
Pocono Ghosts, Legends and Lore (w/Seibold, 1991)
Great Train Wrecks of Eastern Pennsylvania (w/Seibold, 1992)
Ghost Stories of the Lehigh Valley (w/ Seibold, 1993)
Pennsylvania Dutch Country Ghosts, Legends and Lore (1994)
Ghost Stories of Pittsburgh (w/Beth E. Trapani, 1994)
•

PENNSYLVANIA DUTCH COUNTRY GHOSTS LEGENDS AND LORE

PHOTO GALLERY

PENNSYLVANIA DUTCH COUNTRY GHOSTS, LEGENDS AND LORE
PHOTO GALLERY

Time has clouded the details of her death, but the ghost of a young woman who reportedly died on her wedding day is said to energize this "walking statue" in the Lancaster Cemetery.

PENNSYLVANIA DUTCH COUNTRY
GHOSTS, LEGENDS AND LORE
PHOTO GALLERY

An eerie glow is cast upon the Gonder House in Strasburg. Legend has it that the cackling ghost of a spurned sister remains inside the sprawling mansion.

PENNSYLVANIA DUTCH COUNTRY GHOSTS, LEGENDS AND LORE
PHOTO GALLERY

The Landis House in the Landis Valley Museum has been the site of several incidents which lead some visitors and tour guides to believe a ghost resides inside.

After dark, the wood frame buildings of the Ephrata Cloister, which was established by a German mystic, take on an eerie presence.

PENNSYLVANIA DUTCH COUNTRY GHOSTS, LEGENDS AND LORE
PHOTO GALLERY

Ghosts have been seen and felt within the whitewashed walls of the old Slaymaker family mansion, "White Chimneys," on Route 30, east of Lancaster.

PENNSYLVANIA DUTCH COUNTRY GHOSTS, LEGENDS AND LORE
PHOTO GALLERY

An interesting past, a glorious present and some unusual occurrences add up to a suspected haunting in the restaurant and bed & breakfast known as the Railroad House in Marietta.

Does the spirit of executed murderer Johnny Coyle wander the grounds and rooms of the Accomac Inn? The stately restaurant along the Susquehanna River north of Wrightsville hold many tales within its two-century old walls.

PENNSYLVANIA DUTCH COUNTRY GHOSTS, LEGENDS AND LORE
PHOTO GALLERY

This tombstone, on a hillside which overlooks the Accomac Inn, marks the grave of convicted murderer Johnny Coyle. Stories persist that his ghost remains earthbound near what was once his home.

PENNSYLVANIA DUTCH COUNTRY
GHOSTS, LEGENDS AND LORE
PHOTO GALLERY

Some of the best-known ghosts in Lancaster County are characters in an eternal drama played out inside the ancient, ornate walls of the Fulton Opera House in downtown Lancaster.

PENNSYLVANIA DUTCH COUNTRY
GHOSTS, LEGENDS AND LORE
PHOTO GALLERY

The "Peanut Heaven" upper balcony of the Fulton Opera House is so spooky, some technicians refuse to work there alone.

For many years, a white phantom has been reported hovering in the seats and stage of the Fulton Opera House.

PENNSYLVANIA DUTCH COUNTRY GHOSTS, LEGENDS AND LORE
PHOTO GALLERY

Check the third floor windows of what is now part of Bube's Brewery restaurant complex in Mt. Joy. Do you see the ghost of a young woman peering from on high? People say her spirit is among those which occupy the deep catacombs and Victorian rooms of the old hotel and brewery.

PENNSYLVANIA DUTCH COUNTRY GHOSTS, LEGENDS AND LORE
PHOTO GALLERY

Sam Allen, proprietor of Bube's Brewery and Catacombs, readily reveals the legends of the lantern-lit depths of the dark chambers and passageways deep beneath the streets of Mt. Joy.

The faint aroma of roses and other unexplained occurrences have led the proprietor of the Alden House in Lititz to speculate that the bed and breakfast inn may be haunted by a benevolent spirit.

PENNSYLVANIA DUTCH COUNTRY GHOSTS, LEGENDS AND LORE
PHOTO GALLERY

A familiar legend in southern Lancaster County involves the placement of this head in a window of a house on Carter's Hill, near New Texas. The face in the window has mystified passers-by since Civil War times.